Keith Hill is a New Zealand writer whose work explores the boundaries between mysticism, history, science, religion and psychology. His books include *Striving To Be Human* (2006), *The God Revolution* (2011) and *Practical Spirituality* (2013), each of which won the Ashton Wylie Award, New Zealand's premiere prize for spiritual writing. Keith's translations of mystical poetry include the *Bhagavad Gita* and *Walking Without Feet*, selected poems by Mirabai and Kabir.

Reviews of *The God Revolution*

"Keith Hill is a writer in the vein of Karen Armstrong ... The prize that celebrates New Zealand's forward thinkers is thoroughly deserved." – Mike Alexander, Sunday Star Times

"A scholarly yet accessible book. ... Deserves to be read by all those who care about ideas, the trajectory of civilization and its future form." – Peter Dornauf, www.eyecontact.com

BY KEITH HILL

NON-FICTION
The God Revolution
Striving to Be Human
Experimental Spirituality
What is Really Going On?

FICTION
The Ecstasy of Cabeza de Vaca
Puck of the Starways
Blue Kisses

MYSTICAL POETRY
The Bhagavad Gita: A New Poetic Version
Walking Without Feet:
Selected Poetry of Mirabai and Kabir
Psalms of Exile and Return

WITH PETER CALVERT
The Matapaua Conversations
The Kosmic Web

The New Mysticism

How scientific and religious paradigms
are being overturned by daring explorers
revealing hidden aspects of reality

Keith Hill

First published by Attar Books 2017
Copyright © Keith Hill 2017
The moral rights of the author have been asserted

Hardcover ISBN 978-0-473-39036-5
Paperback ISBN 978-0-473-36933-0
Ebook ISBN 978-0-473-36934-7

Cover design by www.damonza.com

Attar Books
www.attarbooks.com

Contents

THE SCOPE OF NEW MYSTICISM

The State of Mysticism Today

CHAPTER ONE

Clapping With Two Hands

I DIDN'T KNOW WHERE I WAS GOING. When I asked for directions at the Merta City bus terminal a guy waved vaguely at the dirt road that swung away from the diesel-belching bus. There were no street signs, and even if there had been I couldn't read Hindi, so I just followed the straggling line of passengers as they trudged from the station, feeling hot, dry, confused.

I passed street stalls where men wearing dhotis—long pieces of cloth that circled their waist and looped around their legs—were selling fruit, milky tea, and meals of rice, vegetables and chapatis. Smoke from charcoal fires drifted in the air, mingling with the heat and dust. I passed concrete buildings, their windows vertical metal bars, behind which were weathered wooden shutters. Soon the street ended at a T-junction. In front of me was an expanse of bare ground, dotted with low shrubs and stunted trees, part of the Rajasthani desert that stretched away for hundreds of kilometers. Here the road went left and right. I flipped a mental coin, chose one, hitched my pack on my shoulder, and kept walking. The year was 1979, I was twenty-two years old, and I was in India looking for a guru.

For years after, whenever anyone asked me why I decided to travel alone to a small town deep in Rajasthan, knowing no one, not able to speak the language, not clear about what I would find, I was never able to offer a sensible explanation. The truth was I actually didn't think much about it. Going to India was something I just felt compelled to do. India was a place something deep inside me needed to experience, the latest step in a quest that had begun years before.

When I was growing up in suburban New Zealand a pop song expressed the frustration many of my generation felt about living in a world shaped geopolitically by the Cold War and socially by 1950s conservatism. The song was *We Gotta Get Out of This Place,* performed by The Animals. Realising I was ignorant of so much, the place I felt I "gotta get out of" wasn't the suburbs, it was my own uninformed self.

This feeling, and my desire to ride it into dazzling revelation, reached a turning point in mid 1973, when I was sixteen years old. Hungry to learn, I had been reading everything I could get my hands on. Books became highways along which I raced, intoxicated by real and imagined vistas from the past, present and future, as I soaked up others' insights into worlds I longed to enter. Yet among all the books those on mysticism held a special allure.

As readers, we've had the experience of excitedly turning a book's page and suddenly, click!, what we are reading causes some fragment deep within us to spark into life, pushing us towards what we are convinced we truly need to explore. During late 1973 and early 1974 three books in particular riveted my attention and sent me in an unanticipated direction. This pivotal period began with Carlos Castaneda's *A Separate Reality.*

IN SEARCH OF A SEPARATE REALITY

By 1973 Carlos Castaneda's first three books had become a cultural sensation. During the 1960s Castaneda had been an anthropology student at the University of California, researching the use of psychoactive drugs by Central American shamans. In Mexico a colleague introduced Castaneda to a man to whom he gave the name Don Juan, a Yaqui Indian reputed to have knowledge of hallucinogenic peyote.

After a year of regularly meeting, Don Juan revealed himself as a brujo, a sorcerer. He agreed to teach Castaneda about the hallucinogens he used. However, Don Juan maintained that the way to learn was not via the detached observational method used by anthropologists but through personal experience. Castaneda subsequently became Don Juan's apprentice. Over a period of five years he underwent a series of drug-stimulated encounters that profoundly transformed his view of himself and the world.

To me, Castaneda's first book, *A Separate Reality,* vividly conveyed the realisation that the world is not as it appears, that an aspect of reality exists in parallel to the everyday, from which mysterious forces emanate, acting on us in ways we rarely recognise. Yet if we expand our awareness, as Castaneda did under Don Juan's tutelage, it is possible for us to directly experience that parallel reality for ourselves.

At sixteen, I found such a prospect utterly thrilling. From the ages of five to fourteen I had attended Sunday school, learning the stories and theology of the Presbyterian Christian faith. As children do, initially I accepted what I was taught. But by my teens I had developed a major problem with the Christian outlook. I was being taught that the era of exploring spiritual reality was over. Jesus had done it all. He had been born of virgin, debated with the Devil in the wilderness, performed miracles, raised the dead, visited hell, was resurrected from the dead, and finally disappeared into heaven. What a life that was! I wondered why I couldn't experience at least some of it, but was told my task as a believer wasn't to hang out in the wilderness, meet the Devil, experience miracles, descend into hell, or sample heaven. That was for the sons of gods and was off limits to mere human beings. Instead, my task as a believer was to study the scriptures, do good, live soberly, and patiently wait for Jesus to come back ... for as long as that took.

Personally, this prospect of eternal passivity was deeply unsatisfying. I wanted to become involved in at least *some* of whatever spiritual action was happening. Castaneda's books excited me because they indicated that, even though we live two thousand years after Jesus, the separate reality is still available to us today and we can jump into it if we want. All we needed was to transform our awareness.

But how could I do that? What I needed was more information. In Goodeys, a bookshop in my home town dedicated to spirituality and mysticism, I came across the second inspirational book, Paul Brunton's *A Search in Secret India*, an account of his 1930 travels through India in search of sages. Brunton's book remains unique. It was the first to introduce Westerners to yoga. It also described people who possessed remarkable skills and knowledge, particularly Ramana Maharshi, who in the following decades came to be acknowledged as one of the twentieth century's greatest mystics. Brunton was no wide-eyed pushover. He strove to be open-minded and non-judgemental, but he was also alert to humbug and sought to maintain a level-headed and rational approach when dealing with the often strange people and phenomena he encountered. During his travels Brunton met astrologers, philosophers, magicians, yogis, and self-professed messiahs. Accordingly, I realised that Don Juan wasn't the only person who knew about the separate reality. There were many, many more.

A Search in Secret India led me to the realisation that I needed guidance. Clearly, for me to travel to Mexico in search of the mysterious Don Juan, whose real name Castaneda had not divulged, would be a futile exercise. Yet that didn't matter because Paul Brunton's book indicated there were multiple potential guides. The problem was that Brunton had travelled to India decades before, so none of those he met were still alive. At the age of sixteen I was also a minor under parental care, so travelling anywhere was impossible. I needed to find some other way to "get outta this place".

I found the solution in the third book, *In Search of the Miraculous*, by the Russian writer, P.D. Ouspensky. In 1915 Ouspensky had recently arrived back in St Petersburg after travelling through the East in search of what he called the miraculous.

> The "miraculous" is very difficult to define. But for me this word had a quite definite meaning. I had come to the conclusion a long time ago that there was no escape from the labyrinth of contradictions in which we live except by an entirely new road, unlike anything hitherto known or used by us. But where this new or forgotten road began I was unable to say. I already knew then as an undoubted fact that beyond the thin film of false reality there existed another reality from which, for some reason, something separated us. The "miraculous" was a penetration into this unknown reality.

Soon after arriving in St Petersburg Ouspensky was introduced to the Greek-Armenian mystic, G.I. Gurdjieff. *In Search of the Miraculous* describes Gurdjieff's system, which he called the Fourth Way. The Fourth Way began with an analysis of humanity's limitations, then offered a set of psychological practices individuals could use to transform their awareness. In Gurdjieff's Fourth Way Ouspensky found a miraculous entrance to the unknown reality.

Everything I read in *In Search of the Miraculous* resonated with me. When I reached a passage in which Gurdjieff stated that progress required a school environment, I began searching for a suitable school. Within two weeks I had found such a group operating in my home town. It was led by a New Zealander who blended Gurdjieff's Fourth Way with spiritual teachings drawn from Buddhism, Indian mysticism and Sufism. I joined in 1975. The group provided me with a highly stimulating learning environment for the next fourteen years.

Everyone finds the miraculous in their own way. Books provided my path. *A Separate Reality* revealed that an alternative reality exists, from *A Search in Secret India* I learned there are many ways to transform awareness to access that reality, and *In Search of the Miraculous* led me to a suitable practical method for transforming my own awareness.

But was this actually the case? Concerned people tried to persuade me that I wasn't on a journey of discovery but, as a mere teenager, I was instead being taken for a ride. It's a widespread and justified fear. Paul Brunton met people who impressed him as highly capable fakirs; others he found were fakers. But in his later years Brunton was himself accused of being a false guru. Similarly, Ouspensky was criticised for losing his mojo in his final decades, while Castaneda and Gurdjieff have tarnished reputations, with critics describing each as a charlatan whose greatest ability was to exploit the vulnerable.

As I walked through the streets of Merta City the question that kept coming back to me was what would I find? Truth or falsity? A fakir or a faker? Of course, the reality was more complex than this simplistic dichotomy allowed. I soon discovered my biggest problem wasn't that I risked being given wrong answers, my problem was that I was asking the wrong questions.

THE MIRACULOUS AND INDIA'S ENIGMAS

After wandering around the outskirts of Merta, I eventually found the ashram. I hadn't ever been to a Christian monastery, let alone an Indian ashram, so I had few expectations. But I didn't think I would find battered iron gates so nondescript they could open into an engineering shop. I also anticipated some level of formality, that a follower would meet me and I would be taken to an audience with the yogi. My introduction didn't pan out that way at all.

I hit my knuckles three times on the gate, stood back, and waited. And waited. And waited some more. I began to suspect that I had come at the wrong time. Maybe the yogis were meditating. Or, worse, maybe I had knocked on the wrong gate. I was considering what to do next when I heard bolts pulled back and the gate squeaked half open.

A man well past middle aged looked out at me. He was slight, had straggly grey hair and beard, and wore only an orange cloth, tied loosely around his waist, which was not entirely clean. I introduced myself and stated I had come from New Zealand. He said nothing but signalled me to enter. So I met Shri Mouniji Maharaj.

After we were seated on a concrete pad outside the ashram's main steps the yogi offered me cool water, which I gratefully accepted, then quizzed me on how I knew about his ashram. I pulled out a letter from a friend who had provided directions. During this inquisition I learned more about Shri Mouniji. First, he didn't speak. He communicated by pointing at letters to spell words. I found out later that he understood English very well but had taken a vow of silence many years before—"mouni" means mute. I also discovered why Shri Mouniji had responded to my knock on the gate: there were no followers to do so. Only Shri Mouniji and his right-hand man Chelaji—"chela" means pupil, "ji" is a term of respect—lived in the ashram. Chelaji was a solidly-built man in his forties who laughed a lot, spoke a little English, and did all the talking to visitors. Otherwise two boys rented rooms at one end of the ashram. They attended a local school, went home during the weekends, and kept to themselves. The ashram was a quiet compound on the edge of town, with the desert blowing beyond its walls.

Conditions were austere to an extreme. L-shaped in design, the single ashram building consisted of a public reception hallway, a kitchen, and a number of rooms for sleeping. Everything was constructed of concrete. The rooms had no doors and there was no furniture. Everyone sat and slept on mats laid out on the concrete floors. Outside, the ashram's dirt grounds formed a rectangle about one hundred metres by eighty. They were surrounded on all four sides by walls well over head height. The ashram had originally been built in the desert outside Merta, but over the years residential building had crept out, and now lanes and squat concrete houses ran along two of the ashram's walls. The only greenery inside the grounds was a small vegetable garden and a eucalyptus tree donated by one of Mouniji's Australian pupils. There was also a shower block and a septic tank toilet. The desert beyond was dry and hot, and when winds blew dust flew everywhere.

After Mouniji had consented to my staying he showed me to the small room where I was to sleep. I remember putting down my pack, looking at the concrete walls and the thin dust-covered sleeping mat on the floor, and wondering if I had made a mistake. Could this really be a place where I could find the miraculous that would lead me to the separate reality? What I didn't know was that the starkness of the physical conditions belied the richness of the experiences I was about to undergo and that they would topple key foundations that supported what I thought constituted reality.

MEETING THE MIRACULOUS

Several days after arriving a knock rang out from the ashram gate. A taxi driver had arrived. Chelaji told me I was to accompany him. In town we picked up three other men, travelled a short distance through the streets, then stopped at a shop. One of the men went in and soon returned carrying a bottle of whiskey. As we drove out of town I became confused. Were we travelling into the countryside to drink? Is that what sadhus in India did? No one spoke English, so I only found out what our journey's real purpose was an hour later, as we pulled up outside a small complex of buildings. The complex housed a temple.

Barely a dozen people were present, so we had only a short wait before it was our turn to make an offering.

The shrine was a three-sided alcove, inside which was a statue that had a body, face, and eyes, but no mouth. The shrine's priest—I assumed he was a priest, although he wore street clothes rather than robes and appeared somewhat bored by the whole process—took the bottle of whiskey we had brought. He opened it and poured whiskey into a small cup. After muttering a short prayer he lifted the cup to the statue's head and held it up, above shoulder height, where a mouth would be if the statue's face had one. After a few seconds he lowered the cup. It was empty.

Really? That would be anyone's natural reaction. The priest's sleeves were pulled up above his elbows, showing he had no tube to surreptitiously suck up the whiskey. The statue had no mouth, and therefore there was no hole for a tube to be inside the statue with someone sucking madly on the other end.

I watched closely as the priest filled up the cup again, held it up for a few seconds, then lowered it. Once more the whiskey had been sucked away. A third time the same action was repeated. However, this time when the priest lowered the cup only half the liquid had been taken. Chelaji nudged me and said, "Two halb." He meant that the statue only ever "drank" two and a half cups of whiskey. No less, no more. The priest replaced the lid on the bottle and gave it back to us. The ceremony was over.

I found out later the bottle had to be unopened, otherwise it was rejected, and that only good quality whiskey was accepted. Fair enough. If you're drinking copious amounts of whiskey each day, you want the good stuff, right? As we bounced along the road back to the ashram I was left to ponder what I had witnessed. What had "drunk" the whiskey? Was a spirit of some kind slurping it up? What *really* happened?

Another puzzling event occurred soon after. Late one morning a man arrived at the ashram. He had heard that a Westerner was in town and wanted to show me what he could do. There was nothing remarkable about him except he talked flat out. He began by showing his credentials. Unfolding a newspaper article, he described how he had once stopped a train using mental concentration so a politician could climb on board and keep his schedule. The newspaper article confirmed what he claimed. Next the visitor asked for a metal wok to be brought out from the kitchen. He placed the wok upside down on the concrete floor and tapped it with a small piece of charcoal while repeating a short phrase several times. He then lifted the wok and revealed that underneath it was a bunch of bananas.

I had watched carefully. The man had pulled up his sleeves. Sleight of hand was difficult given the bunch of bananas was too big to fit into his clothing. As we ate the bananas—which felt and tasted just like bananas —I wondered if their appearance here meant a seller in the local market had just discovered a bunch of bananas was missing? Years later I read a book by the Sufi Idries Shah, who described witnessing exactly the same "miraculous" banana trick in Central Asia. He was similarly left bemused as to how it was done.

Siddhis, consisting of physical, mental and paranormal powers, play a significant role in Indian mysticism. Paul Brunton witnessed a yogi who swallowed a cloth and manipulated it so it travelled down his gullet, through his stomach and intestine, and came out his anus. That's one way to do an internal body flush. Brunton also observed a yogi who meditated for years without food or drink. Mouniji told me that when he was young he heard of a yogi who had been walled up in a cave outside Mumbai. Every ten years the yogi's pupils removed the bricks to check he was still alive. Mouniji was there when the wall was taken down. The yogi was alive, but remained in deep meditation. After checking that no insects had eaten parts of his body, the pupils rebuilt the wall and the next ten year span began.

Other strange incidents occurred. One day I craved fruit so asked if I could go to the local market to buy oranges. Mouniji indicated he would think about it. Half an hour later a visitor arrived with a bag full of oranges. Laughing, Mouniji gestured they were for me.

What was going on here? What had "drunk" the whiskey? How had the bananas arrived under the wok? The television show *Star Trek* showed machines teleporting people and objects. Had I witnessed mental teleportation? Or was something else going on? And how about the oranges? Had my desire "reached out" and caused a visitor to buy oranges on the way to the ashram? Or had my awareness somehow picked up that a visitor was bringing oranges and responded with anticipation? Or was it just a coincidence? I lacked information to decide what was actually the case. The enigmas India was presenting me were mounting up. A further enigma was Shri Mouniji himself.

Shri Mouniji may have been in his sixties or in his eighties. He wouldn't say. In his early years Mouniji had been a naked naga yogi— "naga" refers to those who have power and is associated with the snake, itself a symbol for kundalini, transformed sex energy that travels up the body via three channels and on the way illuminates seven chakras (energy centres). Naga yogis are naked because nakedness interrupts the automatic performance of social codes and so frees awareness for meditation. Naked yoga became a fad in the West in the 1990s, resulting in people being arrested for being unclothed in public. In India, there are no such prohibitions. However, Mouniji stated he had taken to wearing a loin cloth in deference to others' sensibilities.

Shri Mouniji's principal form of yogic practice was raja yoga (kingly yoga). One exercise he had undertaken when much younger involved sitting in the midday summer sun surrounded by large fires. He no longer engaged in such extreme austerities. However, when I visited the ashram a second time, in 1991, he didn't eat for the six months I was there. He drank milky tea and coffee, and took tablets to ensure his intestinal tract remained clear, but ate nothing solid. During that six months he lost no weight, and there was no negative impact on his physical, emotional or mental abilities.

On this first visit, after eight weeks my time on the ashram came to an end and I returned to New Zealand.

EXPERIENCING THE NON-ORDINARY

Did the enigmas I experienced in Rajasthan illuminate what Ouspensky defined as the miraculous? Did experiencing them involve me in what Castaneda called the separate reality? One point was clear to me: my stay on Shri Mouniji's ashram exposed me to enigmatic phenomena for which I had no ready explanations. These supplemented other experiences I had undergone over the preceding decade.

At the age of ten, as I lay in bed at night waiting to go to sleep, I often felt my awareness drift up to the ceiling. I was then simultaneously in two places: in my body lying in bed and hovering under the ceiling looking down at myself. I had done nothing to initiate this experience. It occurred spontaneously. For a year the sensation repeated, then ceased. Another experience occurred during my late teens, when I carried out an exercise of praying several times a day. This generated ecstatic feelings centred on my heart that lasted several hours. I stopped the exercise after a year because even ecstatic states become boring if repeated endlessly.

When I was nineteen I underwent the type of expanded consciousness experience widely described in mystical literature. One afternoon I was on my bed, not thinking at all, just sitting, when I suddenly felt my consciousness expand beyond its usual boundaries. The best way I can explain it is to use terminology from the Gnostic *Gospel According to Thomas*, which states that we enter heaven when the inside becomes as the outside and the outside becomes as the inside.

Our normal experience of being conscious is dual. On the one hand we live in a reality that exists physically and externally to us. But at the same time we are aware that our identity is internal and that we are looking "out" at the world and everyone in it. Our body and its senses provide the boundary that divides inside from outside. On this occasion, I felt the body-defined boundary dissolve and what was inside and what was outside became a single field of awareness. I no longer had a sense of being an individual identity inside a body. There existed only pure, unmodulated consciousness.

The sensation did not last long. But it has remained with me ever since. This, along with other unusual experiences, including the enigmatic phenomena I encountered in India, has fuelled my passion to discover what reality is and how it is constituted. Yet, while such conundrums are fascinating, they are only part of much wider sets of phenomena. Castaneda coined the term "non-ordinary" to differentiate between phenomena encountered in heightened states of awareness and what we experience in everyday life. Usually heightened states of awareness are cultivated, as occurred during Castaneda's apprenticeship, yet occasionally such experiences can occur spontaneously, as I discovered during childhood.

Worldwide mystical literature testifies to many different kinds of non-ordinary phenomena. Every culture has stories of saints meeting angels and devils, sages rising into heaven, shamans transforming into animals, and mystics entering transcendental trance states in which their awareness expands beyond the usual body-centred limits. Recent testimonies provide accounts of out-of-body and near death experiences, as well as of remote viewing, lucid dreaming, telepathy, and many other kinds of paranormal phenomena. The internet and self-publishing make it easier than ever to share experiencees, so there is now a superfluity of people's accounts of non-ordinary phenomena. The difficulty is how to make sense of them all, just as, after leaving India, I struggled to make sense of the enigmas I experienced there.

This book is my attempt to grapple with non-ordinary phenomena. The sheer variety of ways in which people experience them means we have to begin by widening our definition of what mysticism involves. Basic to the approach I have adapted here is that human experience involves both the material and the immaterial.

CLAPPING WITH TWO HANDS?

The material realm is the physical world we live in, the world we experience via our bodily senses. It is the realm sciences and technologies enable us to so successfully explore and exploit. The immaterial is not as clear. Each of us has a subjectively experiencing immaterial core of awareness, a core that encompasses both our subjective sense of being alive and our sense of personal identity.

How our sense of subjectively living in the world arises is contested. For the religious, subjectivity is a function of the soul. For the scientifically oriented, the brain generates our subjectivity, drawing on a combination of cognitive capacities, the activity of the limbic system, instinctive urges, chemical exchanges, evolutionary pressures and quantum states. However there is no agreement in scientific circles regarding precisely which factors contribute to human subjectivity or how they interact to generate personal identity. Adding to our lack of understanding is the variety of non-ordinary experiencing. Our ability to enter deep meditative states, have flashes of intuition, see ghosts, know what will happen before it does, or feel our awareness travel beyond the body all have to be taken into account when defining the nature of human subjectivity. However, the standard scientific attitude, that the immaterial realm is imaginary rather than real, means these varieties of phenomena remain contentious.

This controversy regarding the relative status of the material and the immaterial is recent. Ancient cultures accorded material bodies and immaterial spirits equal status. Almost all religions maintain that human beings possess an immaterial soul that by nature is separate from the material body. Alternatively, philosophic mystics have long viewed the material and immaterial not as fundamentally separate but as two aspects of one extended reality. This is seen in the Zen Buddhist practice of striving to internally realise "the sound of one hand clapping". The point is to experience material objective matter and immaterial subjective mind as a unity, directly perceiving inside and outside as one. This is mystic monism, popularly known today as non-dualism.

The scientific community is also monist. However, scientific monism is entirely material. It acknowledges only natural phenomena, explaining immaterial experiences as being either entirely rooted in physical processes. The assumptions behind the monist materialist outlook underpin the secular attitude that dominates the modern world. Accordingly, before exploring the immaterial experiences that are typical of mysticism, three issues need to be acknowledged.

The first is I ask readers to allow that both the objective and subjective, the material and the immaterial, have a legitimate place in human reality. I call this duality "the sound of two hands clapping".

The second is that a fundamental difficulty emerges from this proposition. Most people are comfortable agreeing that we are dualistic beings and that our daily experience consists of the physically material and the subjectively immaterial. However, as soon as it is proposed that the subjectively immaterial includes the mystical, the supernatural, the paranormal, the occult, the comfort transforms into discomfort. It is never easy acknowledging that human subjectivity includes experiences that are not just non-ordinary but are often extremely strange. Complicating this unease is that we cannot currently explain what parts of us enable us to undergo non-ordinary experiences. We don't understand how they occur. This makes non-ordinary experiences problematic scientifically, religiously, psychologically, philosophically, culturally and personally. The wide-ranging experiences that are termed mystical exist in a borderland, between what we know, what we don't know, and what we're not quite sure we really want to know. As a result mysticism not just a complex phenomena, it is a disconcerting one.

Third, the pre-modern religious way of knowing, which relies on divine authority, supernatural narratives, and myths and symbols, is insufficient in the modern world. Today evidence, not faith, is seen as leading us to knowledge. Like much else in contemporary culture, mysticism is being reinvented to fit with this modern need. What makes the new mysticism significant is that it doesn't use just one hand to hold up that evidence to scrutiny, it uses two. The material and immaterial are seen as equal contributors to mystical phenomena.

This examination of new mysticism begins with a consideration of what we mean by the word "mystical" and why it has become so controversial.

CHAPTER TWO

A Brief History of Western Mysticism

TODAY THE WORD MYSTICAL is primarily used in one of two senses. The first is the general sense of experiences that involve uncommon perceptions, thoughts and feelings. To describe such experiences we use general terms such as uncanny, surreal, otherworldly, supernatural.

In the past general mystical experiences were associated with religious beliefs. Today that is often not the case. A landscape may be felt to conjure mystical feelings free of religious connotations. An art critic may refer to work as mystical, meaning it projects a sense of mystery or otherness. Poetry is called mystical when it evokes that otherness or contains suggestive metaphysical statements. Surrealist paintings, poems by Emily Dickinson, and the music of Björk and Arvo Pärt have been labelled mystical in this general sense.

The second use of "mystical" is technical.

THE FIVE QUALITIES OF TECHNICAL MYSTICISM

Technical mysticism is the practice of disciplined self-transformation that enables individuals to experience heightened states of awareness and so acquire non-everyday knowledge. It has five qualities:

- o A metaphysical underpinning
- o Specialised vocabulary
- o A developmental approach
- o Self-transformational practice
- o Artistic expression.

First, all historical forms of technical mysticism are underpinned by a metaphysical outlook. Different forms of mysticism have differing outlooks. A Christian nun and a Zen Buddhist monk may each affirm that consciousness is not limited to the bodily boundary, yet they work within very different metaphysical frameworks. The nun sees the soul as sinful and needing to be filled with love of God in order to achieve salvation, while the Zen monk views sin, God, and salvation as arbitrary concepts to be discarded and strives to empty himself in order to achieve nirvana. These kinds of metaphysical differences apply across all mystical traditions. Nonetheless, each tradition uses an internally consistent conceptual framework to illuminate the material and immaterial modes of awareness.

Second, each mystical tradition has a technical language that utilises a specialised vocabulary. These vocabularies also vary considerably. The Indian mystic Mirabai expressed her understanding in the form of love poetry, using imagery and situations drawn from Indian life. In contrast, the writings of the Sufi Ibn Arabi are intensely philosophic and theological. Where Mirabai's language is concrete and emotional, Ibn Arabi's is abstract and intellectual.

Third, the whole point of technical mysticism is to help aspirants develop expertise in achieving heightened states of awareness. In this developmental context, mystical literature may be autobiographical, describing intense non-ordinary states, or didactic, teaching aspirants how to enter such states. Instruction may be analytical, helping aspirants reorient their personal outlook in preparation for experiencing mystical states, or it may be inspirational, spurring their efforts.

Fourth, technical mysticism is grounded in practice that leads to experiencing mystical states. Practice, of course, is basic to any field of human endeavour. We develop expertise by putting what we learn into practice. The aspiring mystic enters a teaching environment, learns practical techniques, and by practising develops expertise.

Finally, the whole mystic enterprise is expressed with artistry, whether in stories, poetry, philosophy, the visual arts, music, in performance, or via the spoken word. Ideas on what qualities constitute artistry vary between and within cultures, but the greatest mystical literature, music, philosophy and art are still admired because of the artistry with which they were produced.

In summary, technical mysticism is grounded in personal experience. It provides developmental practices that give aspirants expertise in exploring their own awareness. It uses a metaphysical outlook and a technical language to discuss what is involved. And it is all expressed with artistry.

In this book I will explore mysticism in this technical sense. To contextualise what mysticism means to us today, I'll begin with a brief overview of Western mysticism, from the Greeks to the New Age.

HISTORICAL WAVES OF MYSTICISM

Throughout history no mystical tradition has ever maintained continuous momentum. When mystical innovators initiate a new mystical movement they adjust established metaphysics and introduce new concepts and practices. As more people join, the initial small movement swells into a wave. However, no mystical movement has ever maintained its momentum. Over time, each manifested in a series of peaks and troughs. This occurred with the work of the first influential Western mystic, Pythagoras.

Pythagoras (c.570 – c.495 BCE) invented the term philosophy to help seekers journey into the separate reality. Behind his philosophy was the insight that number and not gods drives what happens in the world. He saw number as an immaterial mystical quality, emanating from the separate reality, which he called the One. Number translated a momentum emanating from the immaterial One into the many forms existing in the world.

Pythagoras wrote nothing down, relying instead on oral transmission to share his teaching. This meant that when, at the time of his death, detractors destroyed his communities and killed his many of his followers, direct knowledge of his philosophy died with them. However, one hundred years later Plato visited surviving descendants of the original movement and from them gleaned what was known of Pythagoras' philosophy. He combined it with Socrates' method of self-enquiry, added Orphic reincarnation doctrines and several of his own innovations, and Platonic philosophy was born. Five hundred years after Plato, Plotinus extracted the mystical core from Plato's work, added his own insights, and brought Neoplatonism to its peak. Hence over a period of some eight hundred years Pythagorean mysticism manifested as three major waves. Naturally, because each wave involved innovation, Pythagoras' original philosophy metamorphosed each time.

In India, Vedanta and Buddhism are similarly marked historically by peaks and troughs, in which innovators introduced new notions that had an impact for a period then ran out of momentum. A new innovator subsequently injected fresh concepts and energy, and a new wave swelled. Nagarjuna, Shankaracharya, Ramanuja, Guru Nanak, Kabir, and Caitanya were mystic innovators of this kind. Some waves have lasted for millennia, as in the case of Buddhism and Daoism, and others for just a few hundred years, as with Orphism and Gnosticism. In the West, one of the most significant mystical waves has been generated by Christian mystics.

TWO WAVES OF CHRISTIAN MYSTICISM

Christian mysticism has manifested in two major historical strands. The first is based in ascetic practices dating from around 270 CE, when Anthony the Anchorite entered the Egyptian wilderness and became the first desert father. This wave of desert mysticism lasted a little over a century, during which time Anthony and his fellow mystics generated ascetic and psychological practices and rules for living together. Their innovations were subsequently written down by John Cassian, who was the first to systematically present Christian mystical doctrines, psychology and practices.

The mystical wave initiated by the Desert Fathers was brought to a new peak in the sixth century by Benedict, the founder of Western monasticism. It swelled into a major peak from the twelfth to the sixteenth centuries, the pinnacle period of Christian mysticism. While ascetic mysticism is still practised within Christianity today it has a much reduced momentum.

The second major strand of Christian mysticism dates from the sixth century, when a writer known as Pseudo-Dionysius the Areopagite blended Christian theology with philosophic Neoplatonism. Pseudo-Dionysius' innovation gave rise to negative theology, which defines God by what God is not rather than by what God is. With God conceived of as a great unknown, mystical experiences were defined not as a way to know but as a state of unknowing.

In the late Middle Ages Pseudo-Dionysius' mystical theology was combined with the ascetic practices of the Desert Fathers, providing a yoked practice and intellectual framework that the majority of Christian mystics drew on from the twelfth to the sixteenth centuries. Negative theology blended with asceticism is embodied in the classic Medieval English mystical *The Cloud of Unknowing* and underpins St John of the Cross' formulation of the dark night of the soul.

Negative theology largely died away after the sixteenth century, when Christian mysticism itself fell into a trough. However, in the twentieth century, after the horrors of two world wars led many to question the old certainties, negative theology made a comeback, swelling into a new minor wave in the thinking of theologians Paul Tillich and John Robinson and of French philosopher Jacques Derrida.

THE OCCULT PHILOSOPHY

As Christian mysticism lost its momentum, a third major wave of Western mysticism swelled, reaching its peak during the Renaissance. This wave has become known as the occult philosophy.

The European Renaissance began in fourteenth century Italy, when humanist scholars, led by Petrarch, Boccaccio and Bracciolini, translated Greek and Roman manuscripts into Latin with the intention of reviving the glories of classical Greece and Rome. Marsilio Ficino focused on the newly found writings of the Neoplatonists, Hermeticists and Plato, whose complete writings he translated into Latin. Collectively, these mystico-philosophic texts dealt with a wide range of topics, including philosophy, mathematics, medicine, magic, astrology, and self-transformation. Translations of these texts into Latin fuelled a new mystical wave that inspired European thinkers for the next three hundred years.

The change in intellectual perspective stimulated by classical-era mystical texts can be seen in the difference between the writings of Dante Alighieri (d. 1321) and the later Renaissance writer, William Shakespeare (d. 1616). Dante lived at a time when humanist learning was just beginning. The Florentine poets were powered intellectually by the theology of Thomas Aquinas, who blended Aristotelian philosophy with the tenets of Christian faith, and artistically by the writers of ancient Rome. These influences fed Dante's visionary journey in which, guided by the Roman poet Virgil, he descended into hell, travelled through purgatory, and was flown by his beloved Beatrice into the heights of paradise. Out of this Dante created the first great metaphysical work of Western literature, *The Divine Comedy*. However, Dante was no religious innovator and, while intellectually he was a rational humanist, he remained firmly within the conceptual bounds defined by Catholic theology. In contrast, Shakespeare discussed Pythagoras' ideas of transmigration and drew on alchemical concepts in his popular stage plays, while his fellow poets, Edmund Spenser, Christopher Marlowe and John Donne, drew on Neoplatonic, Hermetic and mystical texts. Their work is wide-ranging and intellectually inquisitive in ways Dante's never was.

Europe's leading thinkers equally found the newly available texts of antiquity profoundly stimulating. Mathematics progressed as a result of scholars such as Johannes Kepler reading Greek mathematical texts. Nicolaus Copernicus was stimulated by Pythagorean writings to develop his theory that the Earth circled the Sun, challenging the official Church geocentric doctrine. The English statesman and philosopher Francis Bacon responded to Aristotle's *Organum* with his own, no less ambitious, *Novum Organum Scientiarum* (*New Instrument of Science*, 1520), in which he argued that truth should be arrived at by observing physical phenomena and rationally appraising them. In doing so he rejected religious scriptures and philosophic writings as the arbiters of knowledge and laid the intellectual foundations for naturalism and the scientific method.

During the Renaissance thinkers drew no distinct lines between astronomy and astrology, magical thinking and scientific experimentation. Innovators like Giordano Bruno, John Dee, Robert Fludd and Paracelsus were free to explore whatever they felt drawn to: from the overtly mystical, to the medical, to the fresh perspectives revealed by mathematics and natural philosophy. Cornelius Agrippa's *De Occulta Philosophia* (*The Occult Philosophy*) was typical of the era, synthesising ancient and current thinking about the heavens, biology, medicine, magic, numbers, alchemy, Kabbalah, angels, theology and much else. Completed in 1510, his book profoundly challenged Christian orthodoxy. Fearing censure, or much worse, Agrippa didn't publish his book until 1523. His concern was well-founded, given the flames that consumed Giordano Bruno's hope of living into a ripe old age.

Giordano Bruno (1548–1600) embodied the Renaissance fascination with wide and deep intellectual currents. He was an ordained Dominican monk, taught theology at the University of Paris, lectured on cosmology at Oxford University, and spied for the English while a guest of the French ambassador in London. Bruno's misfortune was that he fearlessly advanced outrageous speculations, at least for the time, that stars are suns with their own planets and that the universe is infinite. It all proved too much for the Church. Bruno was tried for heresy by the Inquisition, refused to recant his unorthodox views, and was burnt at the stake in Rome in 1600.

After 1620, radically changing times led to the end of the Renaissance and, with it, of the occult philosophy. The Thirty Years War pitted Protestant and Catholic against one another, the English engaged in civil war, and the Renaissance mystical wave not only lost its momentum, it turned into an ebb tide.

THE IMPACT OF EASTERN MYSTICISM

By 1800, isolated specialists such as Thomas Taylor (who was the first to translate all Plato's writings into English) continued to work on the ancient texts of Western mysticism. But the three hundred year fascination with the occult philosophy had largely died out. However, Western interest in mysticism didn't die with it. Instead, focus shifted to the East, particularly to mystical Buddhism and Vedanta.

A central driver for this interest was European colonial expansion into Asia and the Far East. After Christopher Columbus "discovered" the New World in 1492, European explorers reached India in 1498, sought control of the East Indies in the early 1500s, and entered the Pacific Ocean via the Straits of Magellan at the southern tip of South America in 1513. Exploration was driven by the desire to acquire silks, silver and gold for Europe's wealthy, and previously unknown commodities such as rice, pepper, sage, and cloves for the West's dining tables. From 1600 this drive led European nations to establish commercial East Indies companies. Financially, these companies were a great success. However, an unexpected by-product was the discovery of ancient Persian, Indian, and Chinese manuscripts.

In 1783, Sir William Jones became the first scholar to translate ancient Sanskrit documents into a modern European language. Western fascination with Eastern texts culminated in Oxford University's fifty volume series *Sacred Books of the East*, published under the editorship of Max Müller from 1879 to 1910. By World War One, the East's most significant religious and mystical texts had been translated into all the major European languages. It was this nineteenth century scholarship that established the *Tao Te Ching*, *Bhagavad Gita* and *Dhammapada* as classic mystical works.

Eastern mystical writings had a huge impact on Western intellectual culture. The German philosopher Georg Hegel adapted the Buddhist notion of emptiness into that of nothingness, which he then opposed to the fullness of being, proposing that our existence is an interplay between both. This dichotomy was subsequently taken up by the Existentialists, who filled the intellectual void created by World War Two with the twinned notions of time and being and authentic and inauthentic existence.

In North America, Ralph Waldo Emerson and Henry Thoreau were similarly inspired by Indian mystical texts, particularly the Upanishads and *Bhagavad Gita*. As the American Transcendentalists, they adapted the Indian mystical idea that atman (the self) is identical with

Brahman (the Absolute) into the proposition that all individual souls are united in the Oversoul. The Transcendentalists also promoted religious pluralism, helping establish an open cultural environment that led to the establishment in New York of the Theosophical Society in 1875 and the Vedanta Society in 1894.

The Eastern mystical wave continues to be highly influential today. It manifests in two principal forms. One is the objective academic approach adopted by scholars, the other the personal committed approach adopted by contemporary practitioners who study and practise Eastern forms of mysticism, meditation, and yoga.

However, during the late Victorian era a very different wave of interest in mystical phenomena developed.

VICTORIAN SPIRITUALISM

in the nineteenth century psychic phenomena began attracting widespread attention. So many people engaged in seances and mediumship, seeking contact with their loved deceased or with non-embodied spirits, that an informally structured movement called spiritualism formed.

Many occult and magical societies were incorporated during this era, their aim being to contact spirits and revive ancient traditions of theurgy (magical rituals). The best known was the Hermetic Order of the Golden Dawn, members of which included the Irish poet W.B. Yeats, the occultist Alistair Crowley, and Sir Arthur Conan Doyle, the author of the Sherlock Holmes stories and a prominent defender of spiritualism. In France, Allan Kardec refined spiritualism into Spiritism, a reincarnationist philosophy that proposed each human being is an immortal spirit using a series of incarnations to develop itsself.

Other investigators used scientific methods to investigate paranormal phenomena such as thought transference, precognition, hypnosis, and clairvoyance. The French Academy of Sciences and the British Society for Psychical Research initiated the first serious scientific studies of paranormal phenomena. The latter produced s study of telepathy titled *Phantasms of the Living* (1886). Individuals also made significant contributions. Alfred Russel Wallace, who developed a theory of evolution by natural selection at the same time as Charles Darwin, investigated miraculous, supernatural and spiritualist phenomena as seriously as he did natural phenomena. He published his conclusions in a collection of essays, *On Miracles and Modern Spiritualism* (1875), arguing they deserved serious study. After helping found the Society of Psychical Research, F.W.H. Myers devoted extensive efforts to using the scientific method to explore anomalous mental and psychological phenomena. In his *Human Personality and Its Survival of Bodily Death* (1903) he anticipated aspects of humanist psychology and transpersonal psychology that were developed in the 1960s.

All this activity involved equal parts of positive results, doubtful data, gullibility among those eager to believe that paranormal events did occur, and scepticism voiced by those who were convinced they did not and could not. During the latter half of the 1880s several instances of mediumistic fraud were uncovered by investigators—tapping by spirits was proven to have a less than supernatural cause in feet and bones clicking, hands that mysteriously glowed in the dark did so because they had been rubbed with phosphorus oil, and those talking to the recently deceased were shown to be well acquainted with recently published obituary columns. As a result, debunking the paranormal became as widespread as claims in favour of the phenomena. Today's widespread view that *all* spirit-based and paranormal phenomena are faked or imagined dates to this time.

A CONFUSED INTERTWINING

These two nineteenth century waves, one inspired by the mystic East, the other focused on spirits and the paranormal, the latter augmented by the Christian view that spirits are evil and mysticism is irrelevant, continue to shape how we view mysticism today. It has led to widespread confusion regarding what is involved.

University scholars largely see mysticism as a historical phenomena best studied by reading ancient literary texts. They focus on interpreting mystic writings in the context of the historical social and religious cultures in which they were written, and comparing themes and concepts across different mystical traditions. The view that mysticism is a manifestation of ancient religious cultures derives from this scholarly approach.

Contemporary practitioners of ancient forms of mysticism utilise the translations and commentaries produced by scholars to support their personal practice. Where scholars don't allow personal engagement with mystical materials to derail their studies, personal engagement is precisely the point for practitioners. This difference in approach has led scholars to largely ignore contemporary explorations of the mystical, on the grounds they are subjective and not scientifically rigorous.

Contradicting this basic position, a small number of scholar-practitioners have shown that a balance between personal engagement and scholarly detachment can be maintained. D.T. Suzuki and Thomas Cleary have produced an extensive body of translations and commentaries from inside the traditions of Chan, Zen and Daoism. Karen Armstrong writes scholarly elucidations from within the Christian mystical tradition, while Peter Kingsley, a trained Classical scholar, draws on his Sufi practices to illuminate ancient Greek mysticism. Gershom Scholem produced the first Western scholarly studies of Jewish mysticism, and Sufi studies have been interpreted from within its own framework by R.A. Nicholson, Seyyed Hossein Nasr, Annemarie Schimmel, Michel Chodkiewicz, and many others, each of whom certainly had a personal commitment to their chosen fields of study. Today's Western appreciation of Eastern mysticism is built on the work of these scholars, augmented by the practices of Eastern mystics.

Where nineteenth century scholars introduced the primary texts of Eastern mysticism to the West, the twentieth century saw teachers of Eastern mysticism follow up by transplanting their traditions to Western countries. This has occurred with Buddhism, Daoism, Sufism, yoga, and a range of martial arts. In many cases the ancient seed has been replanted with minimal alterations. For example, Japanese Zen teachers such as Nyogen Senzaki, Hakuyü Taizan Maezumi and Shunryu Suzuki, transplanted Zen to North America keeping intact the full ceremonial regalia of Buddhist temples, rituals, robes, and teacher-student hierarchies.

In the case of Sufism, transplantation has taken a variety of forms. Some schools adhere closely to Middle Eastern religious norms, others are religiously pluralist, yet others are not religious at all. The mystical Naqshbandiyya Nazimiyya Sufi Order established in North America requires practitioners to observe Islamic religious laws. In contrast, the International Sufi Movement founded by Inayat Khan openly acknowledges the value of all religions but does not require practitioners to adhere to the rules of any. Llewellyn Vaughan-Lee's school, the Golden Sufi Center, combines traditional Sufi teachings and practices with post-Jungian transpersonal psychology and dream analysis. Idries Shah's Institute for Cultural Research emphasises current psychological understanding over historic religious and social norms. It seeks to generate a wider cultural impact as well as to facilitate more narrowly focused individual attainment.

The Victorian interest in the occult and ceremonial magic led to the twentieth century revival of a number of ancient traditions, notably Druidry, Wicca and Tantra. Modern Druidry was founded in the 1800s as a nature-focused religion. It has its roots in ancient Celtic Druidism, but in recent decades Druidry has metamorphosed into a variety of forms, some philosophical in orientation, others part of a neopagan Celtic revival. Wicca originally involved pagan witchcraft. It was reinvented by 1970s feminists who used notions of ancient crone wisdom to help women who wished to engage with spirituality but without the restrictions placed on them by patriarchal social structures. Ancient Indian Tantric sexual practices were adopted in the 1970s by the counterculture movement, again as much to make a political statement as to foster personal development.

Wicca, Druidry and Tantric sex bring us into the New Age. While the phrase "New Age" is used to tag anything vaguely spiritual that lies outside either religious norms or scholarly categories, it encompasses so much—crystals, fairies, health, astrology, ecology, yoga, meditation, UFOs, mediumship, reincarnation, channelling, alternative histories and archaeology—that in practice New Age is not a coherent term.

In conclusion, it may be said that in the twenty-first century our view of spirituality in general, and of mysticism in particular, derives from a combination of nineteenth century scholarship, Eastern forms of spirituality transformed in the twentieth century to fit Western cultural norms, and personal enthusiasms filtered through a jumble of New Age beliefs. The result is an intertwining of many diverse and often contradictory perspectives coloured by professional and personal agendas.

One additional issue adds a final garnish to this potpourri. While many spiritual explorers do not object to being called New Age, those possessing a sceptical outlook often use the term New Age—along with related designations such as mystical, occult and paranormal—as terms of derision. I personally experienced this at university. I was buying *The Roscicrucian Enlightenment*, a study of the occult philosophy by Frances Yates. As I stood in line waiting to pay I found myself standing beside one of my professors. When he saw what I was buying he commented that it was an interesting book. "But," he observed of Frances Yates, "she's mad, of course." Why mad? Because the occult is beyond the intellectual bounds defined by academia. Anyone interested in the occult could only be mad—even if that individual was an honoured Renaissance scholar.

Academia is one source of the current denigration of mysticism. Others are religion and the sciences.

CHAPTER THREE

The Problem With Mysticism

THE DALAI LAMA is an open-minded and humane representative of modern Tibetan Buddhism. He is a mystic but keeps his feet firmly grounded in the world. He advocates internationally for religious tolerance and his fascination with the sciences has led him to establish a school where scientists introduce monks and nuns to the latest discoveries. With the exception of Chinese government officials, there is widespread acknowledgement that the Dalai Lama is an educated, compassionate man and a liberal force for good in the world.

Yet in 2006 the Dalai Lama created a storm of controversy. The controversy is significant because it reflects a major issue that limits the appreciation of mysticism today.

THE DALAI LAMA STIRS ANGRY SCIENTISTS

In 2002 Richard Davidson, a meditator as well as a neuroscientist working at the University of Wisconsin-Madison, began studying the physical impact meditation has on the brain. The Dalai Lama organised for a number of long-time meditators from among his retinue to be experimental subjects. Through his research Davidson discovered significant changes to the meditators' brain structure.

The trouble began when Davidson suggested the Dalai Lama address the 2006 conference of the United States' Society of Neurosciences in relation to the study. Once word went out a number of scientists strongly objected, some to the extent of calling for a boycott of the conference. Others proposed withdrawing papers on the basis that education separated science and religion and they did not want a religious presence at a scientific meeting.

In the end, the Dalai Lama did give his speech. The problem may have in part been politically motivated, because several objecting scientists were Chinese nationals. Yet the issue was also philosophical. The scientists assumed that mysticism is religious. What they were not aware of was that mysticism and religion have never been identical activities, nor did they appreciate the extent to which the relationship between mystics and orthodox religious believers has been fractious.

JUMPING THE FENCE VS RELIGIOUS ORTHODOXY

Historically, mystics have lived in religious communities. However, a fundamental difference in approach separated mystics from the orthodox. While orthodox believers were content to wait for a revelation of the transcendent in the afterlife, mystics sought to experience the transcendent before they died.

This difference in orientation generated considerable friction. Religious authorities were often concerned that the mystics among them were roaming the doctrinal wilds, beyond the fences erected to mark the limits of what was religiously acceptable. Over-enthusiastic mystics who "jumped the fence" were seen as theologically suspect. Some were even put to death. An example of the last occurred in ninth century Persia, when the Sufi mystic Mansur Al-Hallaj, carried away in ecstasy, shouted, "I am the Truth." Unfortunately for him, the orthodox decreed that only Allah is the Truth and Al-Hallaj was executed.

Christian authorities also considered their mystics went too far. In the thirteenth century the writings of the Dominican mystic Meister Eckhart were investigated by the Inquisition, and after much argument twenty-eight of his written statements were declared heretical. Today, Meister Eckhart is placed among Christianity's greatest mystics but the twenty-eight statements remain censured by the Vatican.

The unease that existed between mystics and the orthodox was not one-sided. The *Bhagavad Gita* asserts that the knowing yogi has no use for religious rituals. The Tibetan lamas set a test in which an initiate was sent to meditate in a freezing mountain cave. To survive, the initiate had to burn the sacred scriptures he had been given to read during his stay. It took a daring neophyte to burn the holy scriptures to stay warm. But those who did jumped the fence and took their next initiatory step up the mystic mountain.

Conversely, many mystics lived harmoniously with the orthodox. The fifteenth century Nicholas of Cusa engaged in mysticism and astronomy, both suspect activities, yet rose to high office in the Church. Many Taoist, Indian, Buddhist, Jewish and Sufi mystics similarly occupied high religious, social and political positions. And at times the contributions mystics made to their cultures were widely celebrated. Three centuries after Al-Hallaj was executed, Sufi Persian poets living in a more relaxed Islamic regime ecstatically compared mystical experiences to drunkenness—this in a culture that frowned on drinking alcohol—to the extent that poets like Rumi and Hafiz brazenly used wine imagery to describe mystical intoxication. We are still quaffing their delightful verses today.

Nonetheless, mystical exploration of non-ordinary experiences has always been a minority activity. And mysticism has frequently been ignored, misunderstood, or feared by the orthodox. Orthodoxy advocates a narrow interpretation of reality. This is equally the case with the pre-modern religious orthodoxy and with the scientific orthodoxy that holds sway in our modern world.

This means the problem orthodox religious believers have with mysticism is millennia-old and rests on crucial differences in attitude and doctrines. The scientific problem with mysticism developed much more recently, in the seventeenth century, during the period known as the Enlightenment. It resulted from ideas developed by the first great rationalist philosopher, René Descartes.

THE IMPACT OF CARTESIAN DUALISM

René Descartes (1596–1650) was a thoroughgoing sceptic. Rejecting both academic and religious authority, he decided that the only way he could know what was true or false about the world was via his personal powers of reasoning. He concluded that all he could be certain of was that he was a thinking soul—"I think, therefore I am"—and that he had a body to act on what he thought.

Descartes also shunned the occult philosophy that had long attracted European thinkers. Instead, Descartes accepted Frances Bacon's newly proposed scientific method, which advocated truth can be found by making empirical observations from which underlying natural principles could be rationally deduced. Among the first European thinkers to practise the Enlightenment trinity of scepticism, naturalism and rationalism, René Descartes is revered today as the father of modern philosophy.

However, Descartes was also a realist. He lived in risky times. In 1632, after Galileo had published a book denying the Catholic Church's doctrine that the Earth was at the centre of the universe, the Church responded by putting Galileo under house arrest and forbidding him from publishing ever again. Three decades earlier, Giordano Bruno had been burnt at the stake for refusing to retract blasphemous cosmological and theological ideas. Descartes agreed with both men—and well appreciated the danger in doing so. The political climate was extremely dangerous for anyone who dared jump the fence of orthodoxy. Descartes' solution was to write philosophic and theological books that supported orthodox Church doctrines, his aim being to convince the authorities that he stood on their side of the fence. However, he also left the fence's gate ajar.

Descartes' way through the gate was his dualistic notion that reality is divided into the two domains of immaterial soul and material body. This allowed him to acknowledge that God existed in the spiritual domain, where Church doctrine applied, but to simultaneously maintain that the physical world was governed wholly and only by the laws of nature. The spiritual world was to be appreciated using Church doctrine, while the God-created physical world was best understood using Bacon's new scientific observational method and rational deductive thought. This separation enabled scientists to develop new ideas about the world independent of Church doctrines, so laying the foundations for our modern secular, naturalistic world view.

However, a funny thing happened on the road that took us from the Enlightenment to the twenty-first century. Descartes lost his soul. And we all became machines.

HOW WE BECAME SOULLESS MACHINES

Aa a consequence of Descartes' dualistic view that the physical world is separate from the spiritual realm, scientific researchers now had a philosophic justification for focusing on unravelling the secrets of matter. This led to Isaac Newton discovering the laws of motion, light, and gravity, which successfully explained physical phenomena. From then on scientists were increasingly able to detail the processes that drive the natural world in ways religious scriptures could not. The truths of science replaced the now outmoded truths of religion.

New outlooks need new metaphors. A favourite Enlightenment metaphor was that of the machine. A machine is material. It is something engineers can put their hands on and thinkers can get their minds around. Machines can be dismantled, their component parts numbered, the ways they interact observed, and the power they generate measured. Enlightenment thinkers quickly came to conceive of the universe as one vast machine that functioned according to Isaac Newton's physical laws. This machine metaphor blew away the fog that muddled religious doctrines had generated over the millennia.

Unfortunately for Descartes, it turned out his notion of an immaterial realm occupied by souls and God was seen to be part of the fog. Even in his own day Descartes' mind-body dualism came under attack. The philosopher Baruch Spinoza rejected Cartesian dualism entirely, arguing that if God is anywhere he must be immanent in reality, not cooling his heels in a separate heavenly realm. Others wondered that if soul and body were completely separate, how did they ever connect? Descartes proposed the soul was resident in the pineal gland and that it directed the body via the natural spirits that surged by mechanical capillary action through the blood. However, dissection revealed no evidence of soul, natural spirits or capillaries. As the French mathematician Pierre-Simon Laplace explained, in order to explain the working of the world, the notions of God and soul were superfluous. Scientific atheism became the new creed. Anything that smacked of the spiritual or supernatural was rejected not just as irrelevant but as backward and unenlightened.

The Enlightenment's mechanical outlook continues to underpin modern science, as is seen in the description of the human being proposed by biologist and atheist Richard Dawkins: "We are machines built by DNA whose purpose is to make more copies of the same DNA. That is exactly what we are here for. We are machines for propagating DNA, and the propagation of DNA is a self-sustaining process. It is every living object's sole reason for living."

In contemporary intellectual circles the pendulum of progress has now swung entirely away from the religious and spiritual in favour of the material and physical. In our institutions of business, politics, media, and learning, while the rubrics of religion are often mechanically repeated on public occasions, real consideration of the spiritual is absent from policy and strategising.

Philosophically, Descartes' dualism, which acknowledged the existence of an immaterial soul, has been jettisoned because as far as scientific materialists are concerned Descartes was wrong. There is no supernatural realm separate from the natural world nor is there a soul separate from the body. As neuroscientist Antonio Damasio observes: "This is Descartes' error: the abyssal separation between body and mind ... the suggestion that reasoning, and moral judgment, and the suffering that comes from physical pain or emotional upheaval, might exist separately from the body." Philosopher Gilbert Ryle completed the argument by asserting that Descartes' soul in its body was, in effect, nothing but a ghost in a machine. "I hope to prove that it is entirely false, and false not in detail but in principle. It is not merely an assemblage of particular mistakes. It is one big mistake." It's a mistake because, as all materialists know, there are no ghosts.

From the materialist perspective, there is no non-material anything inside us. All we have is a brain through which chemicals surge and electricity sparks. This naturalistic explanation of subjectivity sits at the heart of the new scientific orthodoxy.

All this indicates why the Dalai Lama's presence offended the scientists attending the conference. What is ironic about this situation is that the usually opposed camps of religious believers and naturalistic scientists reject mysticism on the same grounds: that it has jumped the fence of orthodoxy!

The consequences have not only proven troublesome for mysticism, they have had a profound effect on modern culture. Philosopher Ken Wilber argues that this happened because of the fundamental change in world view initiated by Enlightenment thinkers. He calls this change the dignity and disaster of modernity.

KEN WILBER ON MODERNITY

For Ken Wilber, the dignity of modernity resulted because Enlightenment thinkers separated the beauty of art, the moral good of religion, and the objective truths of science, recognising them as independent spheres of activity. This was revolutionary because previously the arts and the sciences had been required to conform with religious dogma and holy scripture. Modernity freed the arts and sciences from religion's yoke, giving space for each to explore its domain without having to genuflect to religion. This was the dignity of modernity. Then came modernity's disaster.

In Wilber's view, the disaster occurred because having completed the valuable task of freeing the arts and sciences from their long-standing thraldom to religion, post-Enlightenment thinkers promptly rejected religion completely, ignored the arts as irrelevant to truth seeking, and gave the sciences cultural and intellectual dominance over all else. The result was that one unbalanced perspective was replaced by another. This situation continues, with scepticism, naturalism and rationalism being the default position for today's secular intellectuals.

The disaster of modernity has led to the current often acrimonious split between scientists, religious believers and artists. Scientists view the myths and metaphysics of religion as irrational fantasies that do not, that cannot, reflect the reality of what happens in the material world, while artistic research, being grounded in the subjective realm of human experience, is not seen as real research at all. In turn, the religious see scientists as rejecting that subjectively experienced values and the sense that part of us transcends the physical that give spiritual meaning to human existence, while simultaneously disapproving of much modern art because it doesn't accord with theological positions or with religious moral norms. Meanwhile, artists focus on art-making, largely ignoring the sciences and religions. Or, if artists do engage with the other two domains, they do so "ironically," using "quotes" to indicate they can "play" with religious themes or the materials of sciences and technology, but remain aloof, not captured by either.

This deliberate walking past each other gained extra edge when post-modernists stepped into the cultural fray. They dismissed objective scientific truths as an illusion, arguing they are as much a cultural construct as the subjective truths of the religious. Deconstructive post-modernists attacked the arts by arguing that there is actually no subject, no author, no artist, that only surfaces exist, and that these surfaces are cultural constructs, born in the moment and immediately dying away. Human beings skate across these ephemeral surfaces with no one present to do the experiencing. Other post-modern thinkers added to the tumult by arguing that human truth-making consists of contested sites in which the dominant use their positions to fend off competitors who seek to occupy their domain. Truth-making, law-making, art-making, identity-making, God-making, in fact anything-making, are really just games of status, sex and power.

THE PROBLEM WITH THE PROBLEM WITH MYSTICISM

The disaster of modernity has produced today's culture in which the conceptual frameworks that underpin religion, art and science are fundamentally so different that artists, religionists, and scientists no longer know how to talk to one another.

During the twentieth century the naturalistic outlook dominated academia and public discourse to the degree that it dictated what was an acceptable subject for exploration. Significant topics like the nature of consciousness and the content of non-ordinary experiences were deemed unworthy of serious attention. This situation has created a serious obstacle for those in the scientific and scholarly professions who wish to explore aspects of human experience that exist beyond modernity's assumptions.

Larry Dossey, a medical doctor who has developed the idea of non-local mind to account for experiences that cannot be explained in naturalistic terms, has commented on how he has to tread very carefully when discussing his views with professional colleagues. "I have a physician friend who frequently speaks to both lay audiences and groups of doctors about the role of mind in health. I once asked him if he changes his talk when he addresses the physicians. 'Yes,' he said. 'I make it simpler.' How well I know the reason! What seems self-evident to lay people is often inscrutable to us physicians. We are so committed to a mechanical view of reality that we typically deny evidence that challenges this vision."

This difficulty is amplified when naturalists do not appreciate the subtleties of immaterial perspectives. The neuroscientists who did not want the Dalai Lama to address them lacked awareness of a distinction that is popularly made by today's practitioners between being religious and being spiritual, between believing in a religious doctrine and empirically exploring one's subjective consciousness and experience of being human.

All this has resulted in the dominating advocates of naturalism creating a cultural environment that inhibits any serious investigation of mystical phenomena. But their problem with mysticism is itself problematic because, as Wilber argues, it wilfully ignores a fundamental aspect of human existence: our subjective experience of being human. The result is that today mysticism is largely ignored, despite the fact that its proponents are exploring a fascinating borderland that lies beyond the bprders defined by contemporary sciences, religion and art. As a result these contending perspectives, many people are confused regarding what mysticism actually involves.

CHAPTER FOUR

Contemporary Confusions

THE SUFIS HAVE A SAYING that you can't send a kiss by messenger. A kiss involves subjectively experienced sensations, feelings and meanings—and how can *they* be communicated via a third person?

A scientist appraises a kiss objectively, timing the duration, measuring the saliva exchanged and the pressure applied by one set of lips onto the other. Heartbeat, perspiration, the flow of hormones, can be recorded. But the scientist has no way of empirically measuring what anyone subjectively experiences when they are kissing.

A religionist has a subjective approach to kissing, viewing it as an expression of love. The religionist also projects the values of good and bad onto kissing, maintaining it is moral to kiss certain people and immoral to kiss others. These moral values are considered to be objective commands emanating from the Divine.

Arguably, artists are best placed to deal with the subjectivity at the heart of a kiss. Projecting from what they themselves have experienced, artists strive to express the subjective content of experiences using objectively existing materials.

Mysticism naturally aligns with the subjective approaches of the arts and religions. But where artists subjectively play with objectively existing material, and where religious believers subjectively interpret supposed objective divine commands, mystics make subjective experience itself the object of exploration. In this sense, mysticism involves radical subjectivity. By radical subjectivity I mean mystics treat subjective awareness itself as the object of enquiry. This may sound enigmatic. However, radical subjectivity of this kind is very common.

A kiss consists of what is subjectively experienced when lips are pressed to lips (to refer to just one kind of kissing). But beyond this there is a second layer, in which we experience our experience of kissing. This second layer I am calling radical subjectivity. It is where we create the feelings and meanings we derive from a kiss. It is our inmost subjective core of feeling and being. It is where we most radically are.

Like kissing, mystical experiences engage our radically subjective core. However, where the comparison breaks down is that everyone has experienced kissing, so we know what people are referring to when they discuss a kiss. This is not the case with mystical experiences. Not everyone considers they have had a mystical experience. This creates a fundamental problem, because without a reference mystical experience people have no way of recognising and evaluating others' experiences.

Having no reference experience is like being a child standing in a hallway, hearing whispers, sighs and laughter emanating from behind a closed door, but not knowing what is actually happening behind the door. We have each been in the child's situation. Our ignorance ended when we experienced for ourselves what happens behind closed doors. Personal experience leads to knowledge. But what happens when we don't have such an experience? How can we know what others are talking about? In particular, what happens when those who have no reference experiences discuss mysticism? We get confusion.

Today two principal sources of confusion prevent an effective evaluation of mystical experiences. They are grounded in the sciences and in academia.

CHEMICALS GURGLING, SYNAPSES FLASHING

When is a kiss not a kiss? When it is observed by a scientific naturalist. Subjectively, the meeting of lips involves social ritual or maternal, paternal, fraternal, filial or sexual love. But for the naturalist a kiss involves gurgling chemicals, zinging hormones, pumping capillaries, and electrical charges flashing between synapses. The radically subjective content of the kiss—what those kissing experience from their side of the kiss—is ignored because it is not able to be measured.

The result is that the naturalist investigator is dawdling in the hallway, ignoring what is being subjectively experienced inside the room that is radically subjective experience. But this isn't all. The extreme naturalist insists that there is no room. There is only the hallway, that is, there is only physicality. Such an approach assumes that whatever we subjectively perceive, feel or think is merely an epiphenomenon of our body's nervous system and its brain. So all the meanings we construct about the world are really just bubbles of airy effluvia thrown up as by-products of the body's gurgling chemicals and its sparking brain. Scientific naturalists conclude that when people experience themselves as whispering, sighing and laughing in the room behind the door they are actually in the hallway the whole time. They are just imagining they are in the room. And they're imagining the room too!

This is the first source of confusion regarding mystical experiences. Extreme naturalists have no place for mystical experiences, or for any forms of radical subjectivity, in their analysis of the human situation. The result is that if anyone enters the room, experiences some aspect of non-physical reality, and attempts to describe what they experienced to naturalists and externalists, they won't be believed. Their experiences are explained away as the illusory by-products of chemicals gurgling and synapses flashing.

NO ONE IS COUNTING

The second confusion has to do with the issue of what constitutes a mystical experience. Scholars have no agreed definition of what mysticism encompasses and no clear classification of the different kinds of mystical experiences. Mystics themselves are no help, with none listing or categorising all the varieties of experiences they have undergone when they opened normally closed doors within their awareness.

During the latter half of the twentieth century a handful of scholars began the task of identifying what mystical experiences involve. R. C. Zaehner differentiated between monist and theistic experiences, arguing that theistic mysticism is superior. This means Christian mysticism, with its focus on a personal God, is superior to Buddhism and

Advaita Hinduism, both of which have an impersonal approach. Alternatively, W.T. Stace proposed that mystical experiences extend from extroverted to introverted, with introverted experiences being superior to extroverted experiences. Put simply, this means that the mystical experiences we have with our eyes closed are superior to those we experience when our eyes are open. Steven T. Katz has offered a post-modern constructionist critique, arguing that mystical experiences don't occur objectively but are expressions of socially constructed rituals and dogma. So mystical experiences occur only in the mystic's head. His position is opposed by Robert Forman, who argues that something real is perceived, although he agrees with Katz that it is analysed through a socially constructed lens. The thinking of these twentieth century scholars pulls in very different directions, revealing the extent to which we currently lack even a basic agreement as to what a mystical experience involves. This lack is preventing progress in defining and categorising mystical experiences.

That this is a significant problem becomes clear when we consider what happens when a botanist discovers a new plant. Botanists have developed a schema that divides the plant kingdom into divisions. Within each division are classes, classes are sub-divided into orders, orders are made up of families, families are constituted of genus, and each genus contains related species. So when an unknown plant is discovered it is easily placed within the agreed botanical framework.

In contrast, if an individual has a mystical experience, there is no equivalent conceptual framework within which to situate the experience. Indeed, there is actually no agreement as to whether the individual has even undergone a mystical experience. For some the experience may be occult, not mystical. For others it is a culturally constructed simulacrum that imitates what others teach. This situation is equivalent to a botanist discovering a new tree, but because there is no agreed classification scheme some experts argue that what has been found isn't a tree, others assert it isn't a plant, and yet others maintain it doesn't exist!

Clearly, this situation is untenable. Until we have identified, described and categorised all the varieties of mystical experiences, we cannot coherently discuss their full scope. This situation will not change in the immediate future. Botanists took two centuries to develop their current conceptual framework. Much work is required to generate a similar framework for mysticism.

This is a major blockage to progress. Yet before I can go further some indication of the range of mystical experiences is required, if only to indicate what kinds of mystical experiences are being discussed here. Accordingly, I offer a preliminary, necessarily incomplete, outline of the varieties of mystical experiences.

THE VARIETIES OF MYSTICAL EXPERIENCES

I'll begin by defining a mystical experience as involving any experience that involves heightened non-ordinary states of awareness, with these experiences including both sensory and non-sensory perceptions. This definition is deliberately broad. It includes all kinds of non-ordinary feelings, intuitions, communications, and impressions, along with supposed physical and non-physical objects of perception. Types of experiences included within this definition are:

o *Unitive spiritual experiences*, whether with a personal deity or with a formless and/or impersonal presence or force.

o *Expanded awareness experiences*, from mind-opening intuitive experiences that connect apparently disparate events to an extreme expansion in which all sense of self is annihilated.

o *Nature mysticism experiences*, in which some immanent power is felt to exist in parts or through all of the natural world.

o *Meditation experiences*, in which a wide variety of radically subjective states are entered and various phenomena encountered.

o *Intuitive knowledge*, in which one knows things to which one ordinarily has no access, such as what another person is doing, or intuiting another's formative life experiences.

o *Out-of-body experiences*, involving states in which one's awareness is experienced as being separate from one's body.

o *Rebirth experiences*, in which inner transformation is felt.

o *Near death experiences*, in which one perceives one's own dead body and/or experiences travel to a non-physical realm.

o *Abduction experiences*, in which an individual feels transported to an alternative place or dimension.

o *Paranormal experiences*, including telepathy, mind reading, distant viewing, clairvoyance, clairaudience and precognition.

o Shamanic *experiences*, such as becoming an animal or flying.

o *Experiences of the dead*, whether this involves perceiving ghosts, feeling ghostly presences, or meeting the dead in dreams, during meditation or in the course of everyday life.

o *Communication with the dead*, involving mediumship or personal communications with dead friends or family.

o *Communication with spiritual identities* by a variety of means including meditation, dreams, channelling, out-of-body travel.

o *Dreaming*, in which perceptions and information pertinent to one's life are received.

o *Lucid dreaming*, in which people have dreams of such extraordinary vividness and power that they are convinced their awareness is in another time and/or place.

o *Past life experiences*, involving remembering or reliving experiences that have not occurred during this lifetime.

OPENING UP MYSTICISM

What is likely unexpected in this list is that occult, paranormal and extra-sensory perceptions are included among experiences that are generally regarded as mystical. This is because we are in the first stages of identifying and categorising the variety of mystical experiences, so nothing that involves non-ordinary experiences should be excluded from consideration.

Such an open approach is required because historically mysticism has been conceived of as involving either the radically subjective experience of uniting with the divine, in which the mystic's awareness is directed inwards and merges with the transcendent ground of consciousness, or when the mystic's consciousness expands to merge with an all-encompassing divinity that is felt to fill the world. These two types of radically subjective experience, one of naughting the self, the other of expanding beyond the self, have historically been declared religiously approved mystical experiences, while most other kinds of non-ordinary perception has been categorised as non-mystical and not approved. To further entrench this disapproval, Western religious apologists have labelled non-approved mystical experiences occult and condemned the occult as devilish. This demarcation has become so deeply ingrained that even non-religious Western scholars and researchers continue to place the mystical and the occult in different categories and to see the mystical as superior to the occult and paranormal.

This is an arbitrary demarcation based on historical assumptions. Until all non-ordinary subjective experiences have been identified and placed into the equivalents of botanical divisions, classes, orders and families, there is no reason to exclude any non-ordinary perceptions. Openness to the full spectrum of possibilities needs to be maintained—that is, if we wish to seriously investigate all non-ordinary states of awareness.

As for the work of ascertaining which instances of non-ordinary perceptions are delusory, which are projections, which are culturally conditioned, and which truly transcend the physical, that is a matter for field researchers to ascertain once the categories of mystical experiences are agreed and a working conceptual framework is established in which all varieties of mystical experience may be placed.

CLUMPING, NOT DANCING

Ultimately, mysticism is rejected today not because it is conceptually outmoded or has outlived its usefulness. Radical subjectivity continues to throb at the centre of human experience, whether acknowledged or not. Each day millions of people are involved in mystical practices of various kinds. Yet acknowledgement of this remains almost completely absent from mainstream media and from public cultural, intellectual, educational and scientific discourse.

Why is mysticism so widely ignored? Or, when it is acknowledged, why is it so often denigrated? Why is the default position of so many that of the neuroscientists who rejected the presence of the Dalai Lama at their conference? Why would my professor assert that a widely awarded historian of the Renaissance was mad? A facetious answer is that people who should know better—given the range of their education, the many fields of knowledge to which they have access, and the depth of intellectual acumen they otherwise display—have dismissed it without seriously investigating what mysticism actually involves. This is intellectualism that walks with a self-confident swagger, its advocates unaware they're wearing work boots in a ballet.

A more subtle answer is that collectively we do not understand how our objective, subjective and radically subjective perceptions interlace to generate human experience. There is little clarity regarding our compound nature, that as individuals each of us is part animal body, part genetically inherited traits, part socialised and conditioned identity, part higher human capabilities (which manifest in science, philosophy, art, religion, culture), and part immaterial awareness.

The multilayered complexities of human consciousness are reduced by the materialist to DNA, chemicals, electricity, genes, and neuroscience, the products of human activity are addressed by the postmodernist entirely in terms of social construction, and non-ordinary phenomena that are persistently present in human experience—seeing ghosts, precognition, leaving the body, and so on—are simply ignored or, if addressed, are treated as primitive suspicions and deluded beliefs. This widespread adoption of the naturalist scientific outlook, and the consequent disparagement of alternative spiritual perspectives, limits our ability to appreciate the nuances of subjective human experience.

On the other hand, those nuances certainly cannot be understood using millennia-old ideas and assumptions. Our view of the world and ourselves has changed too much. We require new approaches in order to evaluate the non-ordinary in the twenty-first century.

I'll examine the required new approach in Part Three. First I'll identify why traditional forms of mysticism have become outdated and where that leaves us today.

Traditional Approaches To Mysticism

The Symbolic Language of Alchemy

IMAGINE AN AIRCRAFT is flying high through the sky when a book flutters out and disappears far below. Weeks pass. One day a hunter finds the book deep in the jungle. Insects have eaten most of the pages and its cardboard cover has partially rotted away. But enough of the text remains for several pages to be read and recognised for what it is: a school textbook teaching French grammar.

However, we are in the highlands of Papua New Guinea and the hunter who found the book can't read or write. His tribe has no written language and hence no books. The tribesman takes his discovery back to the village. Bewildered, the elders decide to call on their wisest to tell them what has been found. Some of the wise relate the colour of the ink to the skin of a rare lizard. They suggest the marks on the paper are the ineffable communications of the lizard people. For others the writing is similar to the trails animals leave in dirt. They wonder if the marks are records kept by ancient shamans who used animal tracks for divination. Yet others view the book as a folly made by inferior people who did not understand that true communications are spoken. The marks are thus at best a fantasy, at worst a display of ignorance.

Clearly, all these interpretations are incorrect. This is not because the tribes people lack intelligence. Their difficulty is that they haven't previously seen a book, and so they lack information regarding what the book is for. Without that information the book's purpose remains unknown. Attempting to make sense of their discovery, all they can do is relate the book to what they already know, and what they know is insufficient for them to appreciate what they have found.

This equally applies when archaeologists discover an ancient artefact about which they lack information. The experts can either throw up their hands and profess ignorance, or they can take the same course as the tribes people and project what they know onto what they do not.

When we attempt to make sense of any variety of ancient artefact, projection is a natural strategy. Unfortunately, the result may tell us more about ourselves than about the artefact. This is a difficulty when interpreting ancient mystical records.

THREE STRANDS OF TECHNICAL MYSTICISM

Technical mysticism involves, firstly, practical training that helps aspirants enter heightened states of awareness. Second, it generates records of what practitioners experienced in heightened states of awareness. Third, each mystical tradition generates a metaphysical framework that is used to formalise its practices and records.

What happens when we come across historical mystical records, but we lack knowledge of the practical training that led to the recorded perceptions? Or when we are ignorant of the ancient mystics' metaphysical outlook? What happens is we flounder. That is a problem even when attempting to understand contemporary mystical groups.

Those who attend the meetings of meditation, yoga or self-transformational groups enter a process in which theoretical and practical knowledge is passed orally from teacher to student. These communications are rarely available to anyone who did not attend the sessions. Effectively, instruction occurs behind closed doors. The group is not being secretive, it is simply that teaching-learning exchanges occur in the moment, that moment passes, and only those present know what was exchanged. Even if someone present made a record of what was said, the full inner impact on each attendee cannot be communicated. It's like reading reports of sports games or concerts: no matter how capable the reporter, reading about it is never the same as being there.

The silence regarding what happens in closed group meetings is amplified when we attempt to understand how ancient mystics, who lived in very different physical conditions and cultures to ours, viewed the records they produced. We have to cross a vast temporal as well as cultural divide. Two examples will indicate what is at issue.

THE OPAQUENESS OF PALEOLITHIC ART

Currently, the earliest known human records are Paleolithic drawings and paintings. The most famous are found in caves in Spain and France, dating to between 40,000 and 16,000 BCE. These artworks are situated deep in underground caverns. They were likely created as part of sacred rituals. Children's handprints at many sites suggest at least some of the rituals were initiatory, celebrating key developmental stages.

The figures depicted are predominantly of animals. Very few drawings depict human beings. One famous exception is a cave at Lascaux that has a human figure lying between a wounded bison and a bird on a pole. Some scholars have suggested this prone figure represents a shaman, an individual who intercedes between the physical and spirit worlds. But this is an educated guess, made on the basis that in cultures where shamans still practise they are associated with birds and flying.

What makes it impossible for us to definitely know what is behind the Paleolithic cave art is that we have no definite appreciation of their practices or metaphysics. Without knowing what rituals they practised, and without understanding the nuances of their world view, their art remains opaque. We can draw on what we know to offer interpretations, using knowledge derived from studies of shamanic tribes people, but because we lack access to the Paleolithic peoples' outlook it is impossible for us to know what the cave art meant to them. A similar situation applies to the world's oldest religious records, the Egyptian Pyramid Texts.

INTERPRETING THE PYRAMID TEXTS

The earliest version of the Pyramid Texts was chiselled onto the inner walls of a pyramid at Saqqara around 2400 BCE. Later published forms of the Pyramid Texts are better known as the *Egyptian Book of the Dead.*

Today's Egyptologists view the Pyramid Texts as records of prayers and spells designed to help the newly dead negotiate their way through the afterlife. The scholarly consensus is that the Egyptians were practical but primitive people who were not philosophic or introspective. They were certainly not mystical. Yet a closer look at the Pyramid Texts suggests otherwise.

The Egyptians divided human subjectivity into nine parts: *khat* (body), *ka* (life energy), *ba* (soul bird), *khaibit* (shadow), *akh* (illuminated spirit), *sahu* (spiritual body), *sekhem* (personal energy), *ab* (heart) and *ren* (name). This nine-part demarcation suggests that the Egyptians possessed a sophisticated view of the human psyche. Given they specified both a spiritual body (*sahu*) and a physical body (*khat*), did they journey through the immaterial spiritual realm just as they did through the physical realm? And just as their physical body utilised life energy (*ka*), did their spiritual body utilise personal energy (*sekhem*)? Identifying an illuminated spirit (*akh*) implies there is an unilluminated spirit, which in turn suggests individuals could pass from a darkened to an illuminated state. Is it possible, then, that Egyptians did not just journey through the various regions of the afterlife, but that prior to death they journeyed through various regions and states within their own psyche?

Unfortunately, we don't know what developmental practices the Egyptians utilised, nor do we understand the nuances of their metaphysical outlook, so we can't interpret the nine psychospiritual terms in the exact ways the Egyptians did. And unless a document is found that fills in the gaps, we never will be able to interpret the Pyramid Texts from an ancient Egyptian perspective.

THE NEED FOR SYMBOLIC LANGUAGES

We human beings have a passionate need to record, think over and share our experiences. What differentiates the Paleolithic cave paintings and the Pyramid Texts from most of today's communications is their supreme artistry, along with the feeling they engender in us that their creators were expressing profound visions of human existence.

The fact that we can no longer penetrate those visions in no way diminishes their power to astonish and stimulate us.

Fundamental to their mystery is that they utilise symbolic languages. The Paleolithic cave paintings present powerful images of animals, but what each animal meant to the artists, what groups of animals represent, why many animals are superimposed over others, why some masterly images remain alone, is unknown. The interpretative keys have vanished. We are left fascinated—and frustrated.

The Egyptian hieroglyphs are indisputably a symbolic language, which scholars learned to decipher in the nineteenth century. However, no two translations completely agree. The problem is that the hieroglyphs are poetic and allusive. They also reflect a very understanding of reality to ours. Without the keys of their symbolic language, the Pyramid Texts will always remain opaque to us.

Symbolic languages have a dual function. On the one hand, they are specialised forms of communication developed to express subtle ideas. Mathematical formulae, an electrical wiring plan, and plans for plays on a sports field are symbolic languages, developed to communicate specialist knowledge. Yet symbols have to be interpreted, and only those who have been given the interpretive keys are able to do so in the intended way. Accordingly, symbolic languages also serve to keep knowledge secret. In effect, symbolic languages are closed doors, which only the initiated have the keys to unlock.

This dual usage of symbolic languages has long been harnessed by the world's mystical traditions. In part the reason was educative, because exact knowledge requires exact technical terms. But it was also social and political, with symbolic languages enabling mystics to hide their outlook from those who would suppress them. This dual need led to the rise of what has come to be known as esotericism.

THE RISE OF ESOTERICISM

The word *esoteric* was first developed in Europe during the seventeenth century. It was adapted from the Greek word, *esôteros*, meaning what is innermost. Plato distinguished between *te esô* and and *te exô*, inner things and outer things. For Plato, philosophers and initiates explored the inner aspects of reality. European thinkers used the term *esoteric* to refer to inner mystical and occult knowledge.

The seventeenth century provided a historical turning point on many levels. This was when Bacon, Galileo, Descartes and Newton laid the foundations of the modern sciences. Politically and religiously the period was full of turmoil. The English engaged in a civil war, executed King Charles I in 1649, then decided they didn't like being a republic and invited Charles II to take the throne in 1660. In Europe, the Thirty Years War between Catholics and Protestants raged from 1618 to 1648, ending with the Treaty of Westphalia.

All this conflict required people to take sides. Even after peace fell in the 1650s considerable pressure was exerted on the populace to conform politically and religiously. For those who wished to explore inner things the best strategy was to pursue their studies in secret. Hence it was during this period that secret esoteric societies like the Rosicrucians, the Illuminati, and the Society of Unknown Philosophers were established—although the last is not unknown any more, as it has its own Facebook page!

The seventeenth century philosopher and writer, John Toland, was not a mystic, but he was one of the first to distinguish between exoteric thinking, which he defined as publicly shared discussion, and esoteric thinking, private thoughts he shared with his intimate circle. A controversial freethinker, Toland advocated for religious tolerance and political freedoms. He shared his views by meeting discretely with fellow freethinkers in taverns and coffee houses, and secretly in private homes. Esoteric mystical groups of the time used the same strategy, meeting in private and writing in symbolic languages that could only be interpreted by the initiated.

THE USES OF MYSTIC INITIATION

Religious initiation involves taking vows and enacting a physical ritual such as being baptised. Mystic initiation occurs as a consequence of inner training. Initiation in an esoteric sense involves mastering the symbolic language used by the tradition into which the aspirant is being initiated. Initiates become adepts when they develop mastery. Mastery is achieved when technical terms are internalised, which results in self-transformation. Self-transformation leads to higher states of awareness, in which aspects of the separate reality are perceived.

This means that anyone can read a mystical text, but without having the esoteric keys the text's inner depths remain closed. Initiation provides the keys to interpretation. Personal insights further unlock esoteric texts. Our difficulty today with cave art and Egyptian hieroglyphs can be reframed in these terms: because we have not been initiated into the symbolic languages used to create works like the Paleolithic cave paintings and the Pyramid Texts, we view them from outside and are unable to access their depths. Accordingly, when approaching mystical records it is necessary to distinguish between the inner and outer levels of meaning. Only by examining mystical records on their own terms, from their inner perspective, is it possible to understand the works' intent. Doing so requires us to "jump the fence" of what we know and to enter what we don't.

What happens when we are not willing to do so, such as when scholars do not shift from an objective to a subjective perspective? Then mystical records are not just misunderstood, they become the focus of widespread derision, as occurred with the esoteric language of alchemy.

ALCHEMY AS A MYSTIC QUEST

Picture a room bisected by two waist-high wooden benches. In one corner glows an iron furnace. On the benches are retorts in which liquids bubble. In a gas-filled condenser, liquid is running down the curved glass sides and dropping into a flask. Moving between the retorts is a man wearing a suit, waistcoat, and tie. Another man, also dressed formally, is hunched over an ancient book, examining a series of diagrams and symbols, which include an angel holding a sword dispensing a silver fluid from an urn, with sun and moon depicted on either side. The year is 1673. The rooms are situated in Trinity College, on the grounds of Cambridge University and the two men are alchemists. One is John Wickins, the other Isaac Newton.

Newton shared rooms with Wickins for two decades. They created a laboratory in one room and for a full ten years Newton used it to pursue chemical and alchemical studies, striving to repeat the experiments described in ancient alchemical texts. Surreptitiously obtaining manuscripts via a network of esoteric booksellers, Newton sought to wrestle arcane knowledge of reality from vapours and flames.

Fearing ridicule from his fellow scientists, Newton never published his occult and alchemical writings. After his death his family and friends continued to withhold his esoteric records from public view. Only in 1936, after a cache of manuscripts was put up for auction and bought by economist John Maynard Keynes, and he discovered that a third of the papers dealt with alchemy, did Newton's sustained commitment to a non-ordinary view of reality come to light. Keynes wrote of Newton:

> He was the last of the magicians, the last of the Babylonians and Sumerians ... Why do I call him a magician? Because he looked on the whole universe and all that is in it as a riddle, as a secret which could be read by applying pure thought to certain evidence, certain mystic clues which God had laid about the world to allow a sort of philosopher's treasure hunt to the esoteric brotherhood. ... By pure thought, by concentration of mind, the riddle, he believed, would be revealed to the initiate.

As in Newton's time, practical alchemy's goal of transforming base metals into gold is ridiculed today. Nonetheless, Newton's alchemical studies led to his ground-breaking scientific discoveries.

THE HERMETIC CORPUS

The word alchemy derives from the Arabic name for Egypt, *Al-Khmi* (black earth). The first known alchemical text is *Physika kai Mystika*

(*Physics and Mysticism,* c. 300 BCE) written by Bolos Democritus. Unfortunately, this text is lost because, in response to rioting in 292 CE, the Roman Emperor Diocletian had all esoteric texts burned. The earliest surviving alchemical manuscript is *Cheirokmeta* written by Zosimos of Panopolis (c. 270–330 CE).

Zosimos quotes from Bolos' text and from the lost writings of Maria the Jewess, who Zosimos credited with developing the tribokos, which was used for distilling fluids, and the kerotakis, in which substances are heated and the fumes drawn off. The bain-marie (double boiler) used in both alchemy and today's kitchens was named after her.

From its beginning, and as the title of Bolos' book makes clear, alchemy involved mystical transformation as much as physical experimentation. The mystical foundations of alchemy are primarily found in the Hermetic literature, Greek writings that drew on many sources, including Platonic and Pythagorean philosophy, Empedocles' notion of four elements (earth, air, fire, water), Stoic psychology, astrology, theurgy (ritual magic), Persian and Zoroastrian mysticism, gymnosophy (the Greek word for yoga), and salvation doctrines drawn from the mystery cults. Utilising the most advanced thinking of the late Classical world, Hermetic literature was a manifestation of the mystic desire to understand the world as Divine and unlock its secrets.

The best known collection of Hermetic texts is the *Corpus Hermeticum,* written between 100 and 300 CE. In 1471 the *Corpus* was published in a Latin translation made by Marsilio Ficino, a member of the famed Medici family's Florentine court. The *Corpus* generated great excitement across Europe and contributed to the development of the occult philosophy. *Poemandres,* the first discourse in the *Corpus,* begins:

> When once my mind was meditating on the things that are, my thought was raised to a great height, my body's senses being held back—just as men are who are weighed down with sleep after a fill of food, or from fatigue of body.
>
> I thought a vast being, in size beyond all bounds, called out my name and said: What would you hear and see? What do you have in mind to learn and know?

I replied: Who are you? He said: I am Man-Shepherd, Mind of all-masterhood. I know what you desire and I am with you everywhere.

I replied: I long to learn of the things that are, to comprehend their nature, and to know God. This is what I desire to hear. He answered: Hold in your mind all you would know, and I will teach you.

With these words his aspect changed, and immediately all things were opened to me. I witnessed a vision limitless in scope, in which all things turned into light, sweet and joyous. And I became transported as I gazed ...

The vision with which *Poemandres* begins reflects a theme basic to all Hermetic and alchemical literature: that the mind can access arcane knowledge, and it does so by being lifted to the level of God's mind. But for this to happen the aspirant's mind has to be transformed. Alchemy provided a practical means for achieving self-transformation.

Alchemical transformation certainly had an external application, as witnessed by Newton's chemical experimentation. But alchemy's deepest goal was internal. Inner alchemy began with impurities being removed from the alchemist's awareness. The purified awareness was then distilled and concentrated in order to achieve higher states of awareness. Symbolically, the process was described as gross metals being transformed into gold, with gold representing the highest states of perception. The Hermetic *Emerald Tablet* outlines the process.

AS ABOVE, SO BELOW

The *Emerald Tablet* is basic not just to alchemy but to all Western and Middle Eastern esoteric philosophies. Newton's translation begins:

That which is below is like that which is above & that which is above is like that which is below. ... And as all things have been & arose from one by the mediation of one: so all things have their birth from this one thing by adaptation. ... Separate thou the earth from the fire, the subtle from the gross, sweetly with great industry.

The text starts by offering three premises. The first is usually shortened to "as above, so below," and means that what exists in higher dimensions is reflected in the physical world. The second affirms the monist view that all reality is a unity, that "above" and "below" derive from a single source, with the many forms and creatures in the world ultimately deriving from the single source—"things have their birth from the one by adaptation."

Before the modern era these premises supported a magical view of reality, in which divine forces in the heavens above were considered to create, influence and guide what happens on Earth below. This view is seen in the Lord's Prayer, "Your will be done on Earth as it is in Heaven," and in astrology, which supposes psychic links connect the stars with people and events on Earth. Theurgy (ritual magic) was practised to bring heavenly forces down to the earthly plane. The Catholic Mass is an example, as the priest calls on the heavenly power of God to consecrate the host, transforming physical bread and wine into the spiritual body and blood of Christ. For mystic alchemists the purpose was to beckon the heavenly powers not into an object but into the alchemist's own awareness. But this can only occur after purification. Hence, the third premise, "separate the earth from the fire, the subtle from the gross, sweetly with great industry." Great industry is required because inner transformation requires much work.

What the *Emerald Tablet* makes clear is that alchemy uses symbolic language to convey technical information that operates on two levels, the material and the immaterial, the outer and the inner, the physical and the psychical. The symbolic nature of alchemical language is made even clearer in the concept of the Chemical Wedding.

THE CHEMICAL WEDDING

The alchemist's task of transforming awareness through the psychological distillation of base traits, then purifying and transforming them into higher qualities, was called the Great Work, in Latin *Magnus Opus*. The Chemical Wedding was the climax of the Great Work. It involved bringing together the Red King and White Queen. On one level the King and Queen symbolised male and female energies, on another spirit and matter. On the cosmic level they were sun and moon.

Chemically, the Red King consisted of red sulphur. Associated with fire, its temperament was hot and dry. The White Queen was mercury, the colour of silver and of the moon, and was associated with liquid. Its temperament was cold and moist. It was in the firing process, also known as reddening, that transformation occurred. This was when the previously distilled and purified elements were fused into a higher entity, symbolised by gold. Accordingly, gold was produced only at the end of a long process of distillation and transformation, in which ever higher quality metals were progressively produced. That the progression of metals symbolises purer states of awareness is made clear in a dream recounted by Zosimos: "The man of copper ... you will not find a man of copper, for he has changed the colour of his nature and become a man of silver. If you wait, after a little while you will have him as a man of gold."

The Red King, symbolically both regent and reagent, was the agent of transformation. Subsequently, red sulphur came to be used in other contexts, outside the alchemical. The Sufi master Ibn Arabi used the term "red sulphur" in the context of the mystical transformation of awareness. Ibn Arabi's pupils called him *kibrit al-ahmar* (Arabic for red sulphur) because of the transformative power of his teaching, which helped them transmute their own awareness to a high golden state.

THE SPREAD OF ALCHEMY

Alchemy was widespread in Islam. Jabir ibn Hayyan, (known in Europe as Geber, 721-815 CE), was a polymath as much interested in practical chemistry as in mystical alchemy. Drawing on manuscripts brought back from Egypt following its conquest by the soldiers of Islam, Jabir was the first to establish modern protocols for chemical experiments. His work inspired many later alchemists, Islamic and European.

Alchemy first entered European culture from Islam during the late Middle Ages via an Islamic text, *Turba Philosophorum* (*Assembly of the Philosophers*, c. 900 CE), which depicted nine Greek philosophers presenting key Hermetic and alchemical concepts. After reading this text practical alchemical studies were taken up by several European churchmen, most notably Albertus Magnus and Roger Bacon.

While scholarly fascination with alchemy continued for several centuries, the Church soon came to view alchemy with suspicion. In 1317 Pope John XXII issued a condemnation: "Alchemies are here prohibited and those who practise them or procure their being done are punished. They must forfeit to the public treasury for the benefit of the poor as much genuine gold and silver as they have manufactured of the false or adulterate metal." Popular ridicule followed the Papal decree. Dante and Chaucer depicted alchemists as charlatans and swindlers trying to cheat the innocent of their hard-earned coin. But fairground rogues were not the only ones seeking to make money from alchemy. England's Kings Henry VI and Edward IV sold licences allowing alchemists to convert metals—and no doubt would have taken a healthy tax had the alchemists been successful.

Ficino's fifteenth century translation of the *Hermetic Corpus* into Latin changed alchemy's status, moving it out of the fairgrounds and into scholars' libraries and laboratories. During the Renaissance alchemy not only contributed to the occult philosophy, it became sufficiently respectable for writers such as Shakespeare, Marlowe, Donne and Goethe to draw on alchemical imagery—although Ben Jonson, in his play *The Alchemist*, first performed in 1610, reverted to late medieval type by depicting alchemists as rogues.

The public peak of the European alchemical movement came with *The Chemical Wedding of Christian Rosenkreutz*. Published anonymously in Strasburg in 1616, the book's seven chapters relate an allegorical journey in which Christian Rosenkreutz underwent a series of tests, entered a magical castle, and finally took part in a royal wedding between a king and queen—for esoteric initiates, the Chemical Wedding in symbolic disguise.

THE DEMISE OF ESOTERIC LANGUAGES

Alchemy significantly influenced the development of the sciences. The foundations of experimental chemistry were laid in the alchemical laboratories of Jabir ibn Hayyan, Roger Bacon and Robert Boyle. Modern medicine's use of drugs for treatment was first attempted by physician and alchemist Paracelsus. As already noted, the revered father of modern science is the dedicated Hermeticist and alchemist Isaac Newton. In their search to reveal the hidden roots of nature, each adopted a mystical Hermetic approach, seeking to connect above and below and within and without in order to identify the laws that structure reality.

During the Renaissance alchemical terminology was combined with terms developed by Hermeticists and Neoplatonic philosophers to create a rich symbolic esoteric language. That language and its underlying concepts shaped the occult philosophy and stimulated enquiring minds from the late Middle Ages to the eighteenth century. Its influence came to an end when post-Enlightenment thinkers replaced the mystical symbolic languages they had inherited with new symbolic languages, different but equally arcane: the languages of mathematics, logic and philosophic rationalism.

This post-Enlightenment move contributed to the demise not just of alchemical philosophy but of all esoteric languages. Once scientists and philosophers agreed that religious myths were primitive fantasies it was no longer possible for serious thinkers to use ancient esoteric symbolic languages while interrogating reality.

Any lingering desire to present mystical knowledge in complex symbolic form was finished off by liberal democracy. With church and state separated, all citizens were granted religious freedom, so mystics no longer needed to hide their unorthodox views behind opaque symbols. That has led to our contemporary preference for straightforward explanations over oblique poeticisms. Those engaged in spiritual exploration no longer want or need to grapple with esoteric languages. World culture has moved on.

CHAPTER SIX

Self-Transformative Asceticism

IN THE SATIRICAL NOVEL *Wise Blood* by Flannery O'Connor, the central character Hazel Motes lives in a confusion of religious attitudes. While he denies the Jesus he was brought up to believe in, he nonetheless yearns for religious salvation. He's also unsure how to respond to sexual desire. He copes by adopting ascetic practices, filling his shoes with stones and wrapping his body in barbed wire. Hazel Motes ends up a mess, psychologically, sexually and spiritually. Finally, feeling he has no alternative, he kills himself.

Human beings have been powerfully conditioned by the metaphysics and practices of religious asceticism. Notions such as that something has to be difficult or involve great suffering in order to be good for us, or that evil and sin have infiltrated and poisoned human existence, have influenced many generations, giving rise to fear, guilt, blame, feelings of inadequacy, and repression.

On the other hand, mystics have long drawn on ascetic ideals and practices, utilising the traditional religious notions of sin and evil in order to transform their awareness and enter non-ordinary states of awareness. Alchemy provided a context in which inner and outer transformation could be pursued simultaneously. For those with a more inward inclination and not of an overtly scholarly nature, self-transformation was provided by asceticism.

Austerities have long been practised by the religious. Many Christians believed that imitating Christ was the way to show themselves as true believers. So they took on the sufferings of Christ, including being flogged and crucified as he was.

To clarify what is being discussed here, *mystical austerities* are undertaken in order to purge awareness of psychological impurities, which enables mystics to achieve non-ordinary states of awareness. In contrast, *religious austerities* are undertaken by believers to purge their soul of sin. More extremely, religious zealots who bomb their fellow backsliders or kill abortion doctors believe they are cleansing the world of evil. Like everything else in life, ascetic cleansing practices have been applied with varying intents to divergent ends.

Complicating any consideration of asceticism is that today most people associate it with monks, nuns and those who embrace excessively self-denying lifestyles. In the past this involved wearing hair shirts or making self-suppressing life choices. These days fasting remains the most commonly practised austerity. Religious austerities extend from mild to extreme, from denying oneself a favourite food to sitting on a pole for decades—the latter an austerity once much enjoyed by Indian fakirs and Christian monks.

MYSTICAL INCUBATION

The English word *ascetic* comes from the Greek, *askèsis*. However, the Greeks were not naturally inclined towards austerities. Thus *askèsis* refers not to austerities but to self-discipline and training undertaken for a particular end, such as the training of athletes or warriors, or mental training to master rhetoric or mathematics. One fascinating ancient Greek discipline was *enkoimesis*, incubation.

Incubation was a healing practice that took place in temples dedicated to Asclepius, the god of medicine. Snakes were believed to promote healing, so nonpoisonous species slithered across the temple floors. Those seeking cures prepared themselves though ritual bathing and offering a sacrifice to the god. Some also fasted. Supplicants then slept overnight in the temple. The following morning any remembered dreams were recited to the temple priests. On the basis of what the dream revealed the priest then prescribed a cure.

However, incubation was also a mystical practice. In the opening of *Poemandres,* quoted in the previous chapter, the writer described being in a state similar to sleep, in which his senses were passive and his awareness soared out of his body. This is the state of mystic incubation, achieved either through meditation or while actually sleeping.

Incubation was practised within many mystical traditions. The first six chapters of the Jewish prophetic book *Zechariah* describe a series of night visions experienced in a state of incubation. The prophet Daniel similarly had visions experienced in dreams: "Daniel had a dream and visions of his head upon his bed: then he wrote the dream, and told the sum of the matters." [*Daniel* 7:1-2]. During incubation the Jewish prophets were visited by angels and given significant insights.

Dante's *Divine Comedy* begins with Dante falling asleep in a forest and meeting Virgil, so it is in a state of incubation that Dante travelled through hell, purgatory and heaven. Over one thousand years earlier the Latin poet Cicero wrote *Somnium Scipionis* (*The Dream of Scipio*), in which his hero met his own grandfather while dreaming. Scipio was given precognitive insights into what would happen in battle—Scipio was in North Africa to conquer Carthage for Rome—then he was taken by his grandfather on a journey. Flying high above the world, Scipio received knowledge of the celestial realm of the stars and planets.

By the fifteenth century dream-vision narratives had become a popular literary genre. Chaucer wrote three. But they were popular because people believed that guidance could legitimately be received via dreams. Of course, today we see these people as benighted. Yet for the ancient mystics being benighted was a much sought state—because it led to dreams, visions and knowledge.

The ancient Indian meditators discussed the significance of night dreams and visions in several Upanishads. In the *Brihadranyaka Upanishad* (c. 700 BCE) the observation is made:

> There are just two states for that person: the one here in this world and the other in the next world. The third, the intermediate, is the dream state. When he is in that intermediate state, he surveys both states: the one here in this world and the other in the next world. ... And when he dreams, he takes away a little of the impressions of all this—embracing the

world (the waking state), he himself makes the body unconscious and creates a dream body in its place, revealing his own brightness by his own light—and he dreams. In this state the person becomes self-illuminated.

Using dreams to access non-everyday perceptions was also a practice adopted by North American Indians. At key times in their lives, such as when passing from child to adult, or when an important decision had to be made, the individual would engage in a dream or vision quest. This involved going alone into the desert, climbing a mountain, or seeking out a cave, and fasting or ingesting power plants to facilitate a visionary experience. The vision would provide information for solving the problem or deciding on a new life direction. The great Apache warrior Geronimo is said to have become aware of his destiny as a warrior only after his family was killed by Mexican soldiers and he went alone into the desert, where he experienced a vision that told him that he would become a great warrior and would not be killed in battle. He never was.

Did initiation rituals in ancient Paleolithic caves, within which it was permanent midnight, involve vision quests? Did supplicants go there on dream-vision quests seeking life-changing insights? Transported, did they sit among the sacred animals that flickering torchlight caused to leap across the walls?

Similarly, the afterlife journey depicted in the Pyramid Texts suggests a series of dream visions. Did mystic journeys take place deep within pyramids, in the human-constructed darkness? Were the meetings with gods depicted on the interior walls indicative of subjective states and challenges that occurred when initiates explored their own subjective awareness? Did they enter sleep, death's image, and go on extraordinary mystical journeys?

We can neither affirm nor deny such suggestions because we lack information about what actually occurred in those places so long ago. But something deep is likely to have occurred, because the pattern of removing oneself for a period from everyday life, entering a place considered sacred, and engaging in askèsis in order to uncover hidden knowledge, is consistent across all cultures and all eras. Such ascetic practices likely had their origins in the askèsis of ancient shamans.

SHAMANIC ORIGINS OF ASKÈSIS

Shamans have been traced back thousands of years, to the pastoral tribes of the southern Russian steppes, and likely reach back millennia earlier to the Paleolithic hunter-gatherers. Practising fasting, chanting, drumming and dancing, ingesting plants that promote hallucinations, and spending periods alone in deserts, mountains, forests and caves, shamans entered non-ordinary states of awareness in which they discovered what had made people ill and what would cure them. In such states they guided the newly dead to their next place of dwelling, received guiding visions, and found answers to troubling questions. Ecstatic journeying, divination, healing and insights are aspects of a varied but consistent body of shamanic practice that connected this world with the spiritual domain.

Religious historian Mircea Eliade observed that shamans were frequently called to their role via dreams. Their initiation required them to pass through a series of tests that dismantled and reorganised their psychological makeup. This internal reorganisation was symbolised by an incubation process in which the trainee shaman felt, in dream, that he or she was cut up and the inner organs were removed, washed, then put back in place. When the initiated shaman woke he or she then possessed a newly constituted awareness and had an enhanced capacity to perceive at a non-everyday level. As for alchemists, askèsis was undertaken by shamans to purify their awareness in order to achieve self-transformation.

Here, again, we must differentiate between the different uses of purification. In the temples of Asclepius, the sick were given purification rituals to carry out on the basis of what they perceived in their dreams. So askèsis occurred *at the end of the incubation process*. In contrast, for those who sought mystic knowledge, whether they were Siberian shamans, North American Indians, or philosophers from the classical Greek and Roman eras, *trainees began with askèsis*. Only after practising ascetic disciplines for an extended period were they able to achieve altered states of awareness that gave them access to hidden knowledge.

In the shamanic process, practice led to purification, purification facilitated the reorganisation of the trainee's psychospiritual makeup (organs symbolically cut out, purified and replaced), inner transformation promoted states of non-everyday awareness, and heightened awareness led to knowledge. A vivid example is provided by the alchemist Zosimos who recorded an incubation dream that depicted exactly this process. In his dream he met a priest who told him:

> Casting away the coarseness of the body, and consecrated priest by necessity, I am made perfect as a spirit... I am Aion, the priest of the sanctuaries, and I have submitted myself to an unendurable torment. For there came one in haste at early morning, who overpowered me and pierced me through with a sword, and dismembered me in accordance with the rule of harmony. And he drew off the skin of my head with the sword he was holding, and mingled the bones with the pieces of flesh, and caused them to be burned with the fire that he held in his hand, till I perceived by the transformation of the body that I had become spirit.

This is how the shaman is transformed. Zosimos says the priest found the process a torment—which is understandable given that what is undertaken is the complete internal reorganisation not just of one's perceptual matrix, but also of one's identity. Even for those who enthusiastically seek it, it is a traumatic undertaking.

Over time many varieties of self-transformative ascetic practices were developed by mystics in different cultures. In India yogis manipulated their body to reorganise the flow of energy and so enhance perceptions. One simple yogic practice is closing one's eyes. This is the askèsis of meditation described in the *Bhagavad Gita*, during which attention is directed back towards atman, the core of each individual's subjective awareness:

The disciplined yogi, living in seclusion,
alone, devoid of desires and possessions,
should focus attention on atman within.
Renouncing desires born of worldly thinking,
restraining his senses which would grab all around,
mind controlled by the power of his will,
by degrees, he resolutely quietens within.
Mind fixed on atman, he does not think at all.
Supreme bliss arrives for that stainless yogi
whose mind is tranquil and passions subdued,
for he becomes one with Brahman.

Ascetic practices helped purify the meditator's awareness in preparation for entering non-ordinary states of awareness. In India, mystic meditators orally passed on their observations to students until the procedures were standardised and recorded in written form. In the West, the earliest records of ascetic practices are associated with the fourth century Christian Desert Fathers.

ASKÈSIS AMONG THE DESERT MYSTICS

As noted earlier, Anthony the Great (c. 251–356 CE) led the first wave of Desert Fathers. He had wanted to die as a martyr in order to go straight to heaven, but because Christianity was now the state religion of the Roman Empire the lions in Rome's Coliseum were going hungry and martyrdom was off the religious menu. Anthony decided his next best option was to mortify himself in the desert. He first took up residence in an old abandoned Roman fort then, when his fame spread and followers sought him out, he moved further into the desert.

But life in the desert was tough. Many would-be mystics found they were not as resilient as Anthony. Around 313 another innovative monk, Pachomius, built shelters in the wilderness. Soon ascetics were living in small communities. However, groups of people need rules to live by. Accordingly, Pachomius devised regulations, which later provided the foundational guidelines for monastery living. Pachomius recommended fasting, reading sacred texts, extensive prayer, and the practice of silence. He also required everyone to engage in physical labour, growing food or making textiles to sell to sustain the community materially.

Around 360 Athanasius, the bishop of Alexandria, wrote a biography of Anthony. After it was translated into Latin in 374 thousands of men and women were inspired to change their lives, move to the desert, and mortify their flesh. Desert mysticism proliferated.

Among this wave of desert ascetics were Basil of Caesarea and John Cassian. After spending years in the desert monasteries of northern Egypt, Basil introduced monasticism to the Eastern Church and Cassian established western monasteries in Gaul (France). Late in his life Cassian wrote two works, *Institutes* and *Conferences* (c. 420). These constituted the first attempt to formalise the teachings and practices of the desert mystics. Cassian's books presented the goal of experiencing unity with God as being achieved via three stages of ascetic practice: the purgative, the illuminative, and the unitive.

For beginners, the purgative stage involved mortifying the flesh and purifying heart and mind. Cassian identified eight frailties in particular that needed to be overcome: gluttony, greed, sloth, sorrow, lust, anger, vainglory, and pride—these were later reduced by Pope Gregory 1 to the seven deadly sins. A range of ascetic exercises were undertaken in order to purge body, heart and mind. These included disciplining the body, often by maintaining a single position for long periods of time, not indulging in negative emotions and attitudes, serving others, praying, and diligently studying the scriptures. Dealing with the boredom, repetition and frustrations of monastery life, where the aspirant lived shut up with the same people year after year, also became a major part of monastery discipline.

The illuminative stage involved identifying with Christ. Jesus had fasted for forty days in the desert, so regular fasting was basic. The Gospels also recount how Jesus often went away to pray, so maintaining silence and constantly praying was also pivotal to this stage, a practice known as *hesychasm* (Greek for stillness and silence). Other practices involved literally imitating Christ. Thus some, like Pachomius, stood for years with their arms stretched out, imitating Jesus on the Cross. Because Jesus was whipped before being crucified, others adopted practices that were tough on the body, extending from kneeling on the hard floor of their cell for hours at a time to self-scourging.

The unitive stage occurred when the mystic's everyday awareness merged with a greater awareness, identified with God. Cassian emphasised the practice of fiery prayer, in which the soul was ignited with love and desire for God, on the wings of which the soul rose out of itself. This stage was symbolically characterised as a marriage between the mystic's soul and Christ. Losing oneself in God involved overcoming a sense of selfhood, the everyday sense we have of being an identity existing apart from everyone else. Eliminating this sense of separateness involved years of exercises and grappling with doubt and despair. When unity of awareness was finally achieved it led to an ecstatic state of self-transcendence. The fourteenth century Italian mystic, Catherine of Genoa, succinctly described all three stages:

> When the loving kindness of God first calls a soul from the world, He finds it full of vices and sins; and first He gives it an instinct for virtue; and then urges it to perfection; and then by infused grace leads it to true self-naughting; and at last to true transformation. ... And the state of this soul is then such utter peace and tranquillity that it seems to her that her heart, and her bodily being, and all both within and without is immersed in a sea of utmost peace.

Ascetic disciplines provide the foundations for the mystic quest. But they are not the end goal. They are preparatory techniques for purifying and transforming awareness. Just as sports people push themselves during training, not for the sake of training itself but so they can perform to their maximum on the day of competition, so mystics practise ascetic disciplines to train their awareness so they may undergo experiences that offer profound non-ordinary insights.

That ascetic disciplines are a necessary part of training, but are not the end goal, is straightforward. But something then deflected the ascetic practices these mystic monks and nuns initiated. What happened can be summed up in two words: original sin.

HOW ORIGINAL SIN CHANGED ASCETIC PRACTICES

At the time that Cassian was sweating it out in the deserts of Egypt, not far west, in Algeria, Augustine of Hippo (354–430) had become hot and bothered about sin. He decided sin's cause was concupiscence, lust for things of the flesh. Reading *Genesis*, Augustine realised that human beings ultimately inherited that lust from Adam and Eve, who committed the original sin in the Garden of Eden when they ate the apple God had forbidden them to touch. Augustine decided that ever since human beings have not merely been born as a result of the sexual lust that was released at that time, but an all-devouring lust for fleshly things has been passed from parents to their children. So humanity has both been born *of* sin and *into* sin. But, Augustine taught, if we believe in Christ as saviour and resist the sinful calls of the flesh, God will direct his grace to lift us into heaven.

For Augustine, this doctrine was perhaps necessary to assuage his own guilt, given that in his late teens he hung out with a fast pack of Carthage's young bucks. He took up with a mistress when he was nineteen, and she was soon pregnant. It was during this period that Augustine famously prayed: "Grant me chastity and continence—but not yet." He kept his mistress for thirteen years, but was forced by his mother to discard her when she betrothed him to the eleven-year-old daughter of a noble Italian family. He took up with another mistress while waiting for his betrothed to grow old enough to marry, but after reading Athanasius' biography of Anthony the Great he threw over both his betrothed and his new mistress and embraced Christianity.

Augustine's doctrine of original sin had a profound impact on Christian askèsis. In the New Testament there is no word for sin. Instead the most common word is *hamartia*, Greek for "missing the mark". Hamartia is psychological rather than metaphysical. It presumes that limitations in one's character, not an external metaphysical force called evil or an entity called Satan, causes believers to miss the mark of spiritual presence and knowledge. In his *Conferences* Cassian record-ed one desert father, Abbot Moses, speaking of hitting the mark in the same terms as the Greeks practised askèsis to achieve a particular goal:

> The first thing in all the arts and sciences is to have some goal, i.e. a mark for the mind, and constant mental purpose, for unless a man keeps this before him with all diligence and persistence, he will never succeed in arriving at the ultimate aim and the gain which he desires. ... The end of our profession indeed, as I said, is the kingdom of God or the kingdom of heaven, but the immediate aim or goal is purity of heart, without which no one can gain that end. Fixing our gaze then steadily on this goal, as if on a definite mark, let us direct our course as straight towards it as possible, and if our thoughts wander somewhat from this, let us revert to gaze upon it, and check them accurately as by a sure standard, which will always bring back all our efforts to this one mark.

The same advice is offered in the *Bhagavad Gita*, where it is stated that the yogi hits the mark by purifying the heart through worship and focusing the mind in meditation. However, the ancient Indian yogis considered personal effort led to this achievement. The desert mystics certainly agreed sustained personal application was needed. However, Christian theologians down-played the significance of personal effort, arguing that God's grace exclusively enabled believers to hit the mark.

This left many profoundly confused. If God's grace was required not just to get into heaven, but grace gave one the ability to make an ef-fort in the first place, how much did personal choice and effort count? Was human life predestined? Did free will exist? Perhaps freely cho-sen personal effort wasn't even possible? Theological turmoil followed, manifesting in heated debates, tense conclaves, directive sermons, prohibitory diatribes, Papal Bulls, and accusations of heresy. Even the revered Cassian was called a heretic by some for placing too much em-phasis on personal effort.

However, for many believers theological discussions were irrelevant. For them Augustine's doctrine of original sin was simple and straightforward: human beings were born in sin, Christ was flogged then crucified for humanity's sins, so the proper activity for believers should be to imitate Christ and be flogged too. The result was that while Church scholars argued over what should be the proper theological balance between personal effort and God's grace, monks and nuns across Christendom pulled out the whip and tried flogging themselves to salvation.

THE FALL OF THE WHIP

Witness to the prevalence of self-flagellation is given in a letter written by a Benedictine monk six hundred years after Augustine. Addressing his fellow monks living in a monastery in Monte Casino, Peter Damian congratulated them for flogging themselves in the town square every Friday. However, he was concerned that they were doing so with their clothes on, rather than being naked, as was their previous practice. And the reason whipping themselves while naked was required?

> I shall make bold to say, my dear brothers, that anyone who is ashamed to remove his clothes that he might suffer with Christ, has undoubtedly listened to the word of the serpent. And because he was embarrassed by his nakedness, like our first parents he hides himself so to speak, from the sight of God: "I heard your voice in the garden," he says, "and I was afraid because I was naked, and I hid myself."

Here we are, back in the Garden of Eden, peeking through the leaves with Augustine. The story is that after Adam and Eve had given in to the serpent's urgings and eaten the forbidden fruit, they realised for the first time they were naked. Embarrassed, they covered their naked bodies from God's sight when He ambled through the garden, as He was wont to do in the evenings. Accordingly, Peter Damian was suggesting the monks take off their clothes so they would be naked in God's sight, just as Adam and Eve were before they lapsed. When Augustine argued the Garden of Eden is where all humanity's troubles began, he can have little realised it would lead to the pious getting butt-naked like their first parents, then flogging that butt till it bled.

By the late Middle Ages flagellation had become a fetish among those who would be godly. Peter Damian beat himself so badly he was hospitalised, forcing his superiors to order him to give the lash a rest. Benedict, who founded the Benedictine order of which Damian was a member, once threw himself into a nettle patch after becoming aroused when he saw an attractive woman. He was also hospitalised.

Nettle patches not always being handy, most later Catholic mystics preferred the whip. Dominic used chains and leather, Ignatius preferred thin leather straps, and Teresa of Avila and Catherine of Siena thrashed themselves with whatever was handy until the blood flowed. It is recorded of Catherine that, inspired by the Desert Fathers' asceticism, she gathered a group of young girls and had them whipping themselves while they prayed. This when Catherine herself was supposedly aged just six!

Flagellation was then adopted by the laity. When plague decimated Europe in the fourteenth century, pious groups numbering from 200 to 1,000 travelled from town to town publicly thrashing themselves. Historian Barbara W. Tuchman says of these religious:

> The flagellants saw themselves as redeemers who, by re-enacting the scourging of Christ upon their own bodies and making the blood flow, would atone for human wickedness and earn another chance for mankind. ... These bands put on regular performances three times a day, twice in public in the church square and once in private. Organised under a lay Master for a stated period, usually 33 1/2 days to represent Christ's years on Earth ... they were forbidden to bath, shave, change their clothes, sleep on beds, talk or have intercourse with women without the Master's permission. Evidently this was not withheld, since the flagellants were later charged with orgies in which whippings combined with sex.

Guilt-induced flogging brings us back to the tortured Hazel Motes, the confused believer of *Wise Blood*. From our twenty-first century perspective, not only is physical penance seen as misguided but, given that the doctrine of original sin has lost its grip on the Western psyche, we view attempts to whip oneself into heaven not as piety but as a bizarre mix of religious guilt, blood sport, masochism, and, yes, kinky sex.

In the late Middle Ages Chaucer and Boccaccio wrote sardonic stories about what monks got up to in their time off. Today we are probably more sympathetic to the chaste breaking their vows and leaving their order than to the guilt-ridden self-harming for God. In this context, it is understandable that asceticism is viewed with distaste.

To conclude, the difference between religious and mystical asceticism is that religiously motivated austerities are penances performed to repay for humanity's sins, whereas mystical austerities involve disciplines undertaken to purify awareness. Where religious penances are performed out of fear that humanity is sinful and is falling short of the mark, mystical ascetic practices assist self-transformation and help the aspirant hit the mark of non-ordinary understanding.

One significant territory of experience that non-ordinary understanding has revealed is the realm known as the occult.

CHAPTER SEVEN

The Metaphysics of the Occult

OCCULT METAPHYSICAL FRAMEWORKS were generated by mystics when they became dissatisfied with traditional religious metaphysics. Metaphysical frameworks offer meta-explanations of reality, explanations beyond the strictly physical that make some sense of the normal, abnormal and distinctly weird feelings, thoughts and events each of us occasionally undergo.

OUR NEED FOR META-EXPLANATIONS

There are many kinds of meta-explanations. Science fiction writers tell stories that assume the existence of teleporting, parallel universes, time travel via wormholes, and hive minds in non-terrestrial species. In the future some or all these may be proven to exist. But for now, however much entertainment they provide, there is no empirical evidence that any are real phenomena. They remain meta-scientific speculations.

Traditional religious metaphysics focus on three areas: creation myths that describe how the world and humanity came into existence, what happens after we die, and what happens between birth and death. The last includes whether the way we live we lead to us heading upstairs to sit in God's piano patio to choir with the angels, or book us a hot spot to sizzle on the barbecues in God's basement.

This kind of story-telling is fundamental to how we make sense—and fun—of being in the world. Those working in the fields of religion, economics, biology and public policy extrapolate from the facts to tell overarching stories about what is going on, using the assumptions that underpin their perspective. Cosmology offers the Big Bang and the expansion of the universe until its eventual heat-death as an overarching story for the origin and demise of the universe. Biology offers evolution as an overarching story to explain the diversity of species living on this planet. Economics offers the story of the free market as the best way to promote the continued growth of human society. Politicians offer narratives regarding what is wrong with their country and what is needed to make it right. And every nation has its origin myth and stories about people coming together to overcome disaster or threat. Whether connecting disparate facts or taking off from them entirely, meta-narratives are basic to the sense we make of our life.

Meta-explanations often start from actual events in the world—a spring mysteriously appears, a rainbow floats in the sky after a traumatic event, one person selflessly saves others, stars move in cycles across the night sky. An inventive narrator then creates an explanation of why such events occur, filling in the gaps of what isn't known using research, creative thinking, speculation, inherited stories, prejudice, and even sheer bloody mindedness: It's my story and I'm sticking to it, no matter what! Starting from what we know, we wonder about what could be, then creatively reconcile what might be with what is. It's how we make progress.

However, there is one big problem with meta-explanations of any kind. The problem is, how can we know if a meta-explanation is correct, basically correct but with erroneous embellishments, constitutes a good attempt but is wrong on a fundamental issue, or is total fantasy?

One way to start answering this question is to ascertain whether the meta-explanation is top-down or bottom-up.

TOP-DOWN VS BOTTOM-UP META-EXPLANATIONS

All top-down and bottom-up meta-explanations are concepts we generate to make sense of our experiences. The difference between them is that top-down meta-explanations impose an intellectual template on reality, for example that original sin condemns us or that the free market will save us. Ultimately, top-down meta-narratives are not grounded in empirical data but are projections of strongly held beliefs. In contrast, bottom-up meta-explanations are generated out of experience by people who use empirical data and observed personal experience to generate an intellectual framework in which to contextualise data and experience. Indian teachings on chakras, and scientists' overview of how human activity impacts on climate change, are examples of bottom-up meta-explanations. A significant difference is that top-down meta-explanations are rigid and are adjusted only very slowly, whereas bottom-up meta-explanations are grounded in experience and so are fluid, being adjusted to accommodate new data or experiences.

Historically, many mystics used a bottom-up approach, constructing meta-explanations to give their experiences a context rather than superimposing a top-down template of beliefs and language onto their experiences and forcing those experiences to fit. This is why mystics such as Meister Eckhart and al-Hallaj were declared heretical—because their bottom-up descriptions of their experiences conflicted with the orthodox top-down theological template. Ultimately, accusations of heresy don't just involve mystics using disallowed language, but hinge on mystics having disallowed experiences.

When mystics lived in top-down religious cultures, they defended themselves by inventing symbolic esoteric languages in which they hid their meanings so they could communicate their bottom-up observations while staying onside with the top-down orthodox. The Sufis offer an example. Having learned from al-Hallaj's execution for blasphemy, later Sufis adapted pre-existing Greek philosophy, Hermetic literature and Neoplatonic concepts to generate a bottom-up technical language they used to make sense of their psychospiritual experiences. However, they were careful to link their bottom-up language to top-down Islamic religious metaphysics, artistically tying the two strands together to hold the predatory orthodox at bay.

An alternative was to break entirely with traditional top-down religious approaches and construct a meta-explanation using an entirely new conceptual framework. This occurred in India, around 800 BCE, among the meditators who wrote the Upanishads.

SANKHYA AS A BOTTOM-UP META-EXPLANATION

The ancient Indian meditators' greatest innovation was their experimentation with their own consciousness, which they termed atman. In the *Brihadranyaka Upanishad* atman is described as radically subjective awareness:

> He is never seen, but is the seer; he is never heard, but is the hearer; he is never thought of, but is the thinker; he is never known, but is the knower. He is your self, the inner controller, the immortal.

This insight, grounded in personal experiences generated during meditation, led to the philosophy of Sankhya, which placed that personal experience into a meta-explanation that encompassed all reality.

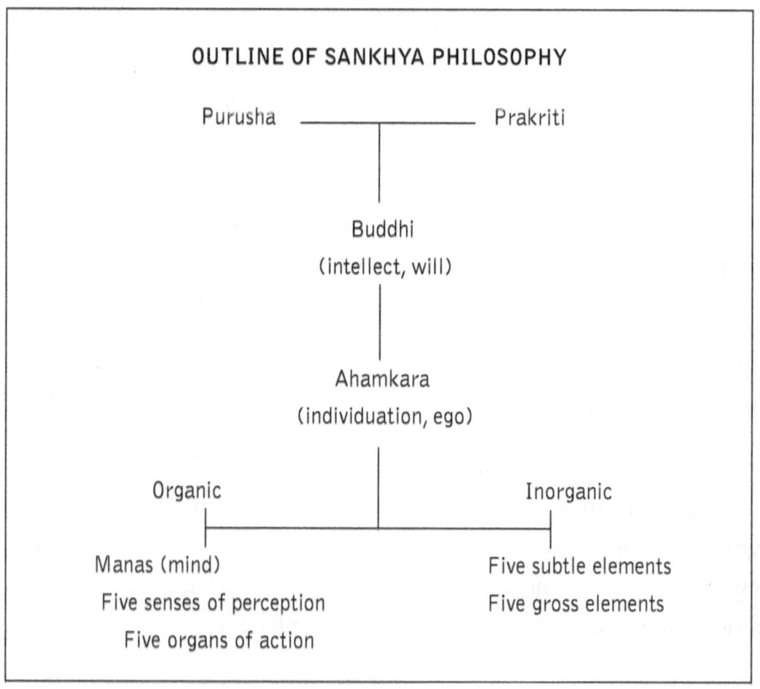

Sankhya posits two roots to reality. These are primordial spirit, *purusha*, and primordial matter, *prakriti*. Both are eternal. No God brought them into existence. In fact, God is not included in the framework at all because no deity was experienced, only the world and consciousness. So first there is purusha and prakriti. From purusha derives personal consciousness, from prakriti derives objective material reality. With this established, Sankhya mystics then analysed how awareness functions in relation to the material world.

Awareness is intentional (*buddhi*). Intention was seen as constituted of intellect and will. Enacting intention in the world gives rise to a sense of personal identity (*ahamkara*). Personal identity interacts with matter via the brain's mind, the five senses, and the five organs of action (hands, feet, tongue and the two organs of excretion). The material world was viewed as consisting of the five subtle elements (sound, form, touch, savour and smell) and the five gross elements (ether, wind, fire, water and earth).

The point is that this is not top-down metaphysics in the religious sense. Sankhya is a bottom-up conceptual framework developed out of experience. As a framework, it is not derived from religious authority—although the Upanishadic meditators certainly referred to sacred texts in their expositions, relating their conceptual innovations to orthodox Vedic top-down religious mythology and teachings. On these grounds Sankhya is an example of a bottom-up mystical meta-explanation that attempts to contextualise human experience using experientially-derived terms.

All this is by way of an extended introduction to the main topic of this chapter, the realm of human experience called the occult.

TANTRA AS OCCULT ASKÈSIS

Occultism has long had a bad reputation, being viewed as involving the supernatural, black magic, deviant sex, even outright craziness. As a result, occult experiences are often put into the "too weird" basket. However, just like ascetic askèsis, occult practices may also be understood as providing another way to hit the mark.

Occult explorations and ascetic practices are subsets of mysticism. But where mystics adopt ascetic askèsis in order to learn through reducing sense contacts and social experiences, occult askèsis involves mystics plunging into unusual and intense non-everyday experiences. The purpose is the same in each case: for the mystic to purify and focus awareness, obtain new insights into reality, and ultimately to expand perception beyond its everyday limits. It is just that where asceticism involves pulling back from life experiences, in occultism the practitioner jumps headfirst into intense experiences.

Tantra is fundamental to Indian occult practices. In the West, Tantra is inevitably associated with sex. There are actually three schools of Tantra. The Kuala school tends towards socially transgressive rituals, including those of a sexual nature, the Mishra school is devotional, and the Samaya school focuses on meditation.

Tantra began in India around 300 CE. It was a grassroots movement that refreshed stale spiritual practices, much like New Age beliefs and practices refreshed Western spirituality in the 1970s and 1980s. Just as the Upanishad meditators had emphasised bottom-up personal experience over top-down Vedic beliefs, a thousand years later the Tantric movement wrested spirituality away from priests and their limiting doctrines and placed it into the hands of practising individuals.

Tantra was rapidly adopted by those in the Vedic, Buddhist, Tibetan Bön and Jain religions. Its success was due to two factors. First it was easily adapted to local belief structures. So while it involved a bottom-up experiential approach, it allowed practitioners to maintain many of their top-down metaphysical beliefs. Second, it offered a personal approach to religious practices that had ossified into formulae and ritual. Like desert asceticism, Tantric practices gave religious worshippers a practical means to make objective beliefs personal and meaningful. Importantly, Tantra provided what we today take for granted: it gave individuals control over their own destiny, social as well as spiritual.

The word Tantra is compounded of two Sanskrit words, *tanoti*, expand, and *trayoti*, liberate. So Tantra involves exploring matter in order to liberate spirit. These two aspects are personalised into the two gods Shiva (male), who represents transcendent undifferentiated consciousness, and Shakti (female), who represents manifest energy that takes any and all forms, from the crude, even depraved, to the sublime. Shakti manifests internally within human awareness as kundalini. Kundalini is energy that rises through the body's seven chakras (energy centres). As awareness is purified, so kundalini rises from the base chakra, through the sex, belly, heart, throat and forehead chakras, culminating at the top of the head. Shakti manifests as energy at each of these levels.

The transgressive Kuala school of Tantra is the most obviously occult. One Kuala practice requires the practitioner to cut the body with knives and pierce tongue and cheeks with metal skewers. Another involves meditating in burial or cremation grounds, the highlight being spending nights meditating while seated on a corpse. For some these practices are undertaken to develop magical powers. For others they are to transcend social taboos and to break down conditioned identity. Others seek total self-transcendence. Within the same practices the intent can be very different, from the base to the elevated, reflecting which chakra's energy is engaged during the ritual.

Tantric sex involves many different practices. One is to confront social taboos by having ritual sex with others outside one's caste. Another is to retain seminal fluids during sex and use the energy to facilitate higher states of awareness. Other practices are more like a swingers' key party. As mythologist Joseph Campbell observed:

> The rite is a form of yoga, a passage beyond the bounds of the sphere of dharma [religious customs]; and indeed, to such a point that in certain variants of this worship even incest prohibitions must be disregarded. For example, in the so-called "bodice cult" the female votaries at the time of worship deposit their upper vests in a box in charge of the guru, and at the close of the preliminary ceremonies each of the males takes a vest from the box and the female to whom it belongs—"be she ever so nearly kin to him"—becomes his partner for the consummation.

Tantric sex arrived in the West in the 1960s, embraced by a counter-culture movement intent on challenging social norms by advocating for feminism, civil rights and sexual freedoms, all while smoking dope and dancing to the Devil's music, rock 'n' roll. Tantric sex fit with a wave of Eastern-inspired spirituality that included meditation, vegetarianism and Tai Chi, adopted by Westerners looking beyond Christianity and wishing to shake off the last vestiges of Victorian prudery.

Of course, most of us view taking part in an orgy with our brother or sister—just to make the point that personal identity need not be restricted by social conventions or prohibitions based on biological connection—as perhaps going a step too far. However, one by-product of all this was that, whether participants were aware of it or not, by taking up these practices they entered the realm of the occult. And, in contradiction to claims made by the straight-laced, it didn't plunge practitioners straight to hell. In fact, the abilities developed and insights achieved often proved very worthwhile.

Historically, the Western equivalent to Tantra was a collection of practices that came to be known as theurgy (literally, God work). Like Tantra, theurgy involved religious rituals and magical incantations, but its practice also required inner purification, and its fundamental aim was to promote experiential interaction with the spiritual domain.

Interestingly, theurgy appeared in the late Classical world at the same time that Tantra developed in India. Of course, occult disciplines had long been practised in both regions. The Greek Oracle at Delphi and the Eleusinian Mysteries date to 1500 BCE, while magical practices recorded in the Vedas date to the same period. However, it was in the third century that occult practices impacted widely in both India and Greece. The philosopher Iamblichus provides a useful understanding of Western theurgy.

IAMBLICHUS AND THE NEOPLATONIC MILIEU

Iamblichus (c. 245–325 CE) was a Syrian Neoplatonic philosopher who wrote an extensive account of theurgy in *De Mysteriis Aegyptiorum* (*On the Egyptian Mysteries*). The term "Neoplatonic" was invented by nineteenth century scholars to differentiate the late mystical phase of Platonism from Plato's own work of five hundred years earlier. Neoplatonism peaked with Plotinus (c. 205–270 CE). After studying in Alexandria for eleven years, Plotinus moved to Rome where he established his mystic school. Among Plotinus' pupils was Porphyry, who persuaded Plotinus to write down his thoughts, which Porphyry then organised into the *Enneads*, one of Western mysticism's most significant texts. Like India's Upanishadic meditators, with whom he is often compared, Plotinus' mystical outlook was grounded in personal experience:

> Often I have woken to myself out of the body, become detached from all else and entered into myself, and I have seen beauty of surpassing greatness, and have felt assured that then especially I belonged to the higher reality, engaged in the noblest life and identified with the Divine, and there established, I have attained to that supreme actuality, seeing myself above all else in the realm of the Intellect. And after this repose in the Divine, descending from Intellect to reasoning, I am perplexed as to how my descent comes about, and how my soul has become embodied—a soul, though in the body, of such manifest excellence.

Consistent with the esoteric view, and drawing on the philosophy of Plato, Plotinus viewed the One as the source of everything existing. He taught that at some moment before time began the One overflowed and manifested two levels of reality, immaterial and material. In the immaterial realm were immaterial gods, that Pythagoras termed number and Plato called forms and ideas, and also the world soul from which all life and movement derive. Below them was the material realm ruled by cosmic and local gods. The cosmic gods were the stars, sun, planets and moon, while local gods were powers that spoke through oracles. Finally, there were nature spirits who inhabited particular places, such as woods and caves.

While the wider populace was exoteric in focus, worshipping the material cosmic and local gods, the Neoplatonists' focus was esoteric, being concerned with the immaterial principles and forces that animate reality. They sought a state in which their awareness flew up, out of the local physical realm, through the realms of the cosmic and immaterial gods, into the realm of intellect where they could experience unity with the One.

Despite the Neoplatonists' philosophic inclinations, a whiff of magic has long hung around them. In part, this is due to the era itself. In the *Gospel According to Mark* Jesus is depicted as a magician who cast out demons, healed the sick through his touch, turned water into wine, raised the dead, and walked on water. The first century sage Apollonius of Tyana also healed the sick and raised the dead. His contemporary Simon Magus was said to have learned his magical arts in Alexandra and was able to fly whenever he felt the whim. This was an era when, to show you really were wise, you were expected to do a little magic on the side.

Among the Neoplatonists, Iamblichus' pupil Proclus was reported to have once used a rainmaking spell to break a drought. And Iamblichus is said to have conjured up two water spirits after his pupils repeatedly asked him to display his prowess. The students were duly impressed, but Iamblichus was somewhat embarrassed to be dabbling in such low grade stuff. He aimed much higher, at the same unitive experience that inspired Plotinus. However, it is Iamblichus' advocacy of theurgy that differentiates him from his fellow Neoplatonists.

IAMBLICHUS ON THEURGY

Iamblichus' major statement on theurgy, *On the Egyptian Mysteries*, was written in response to objections made by his own teacher, Porphyry, that magical theurgy didn't just fail as a means to merge with the One, it also led to errors and false knowledge.

Porphyry possessed a modern rational sceptical outlook. Among his objections to theurgy was that oracles merely got high on subterranean gases or adulterated water and said whatever came into their head, or spoke so enigmatically their words could be interpreted to mean anything. Porphyry also maintained that those who claimed they had access to non-ordinary knowledge were good at reading their supplicants' cues, made educated guesses, or lied outright. He doubted dreams experienced during incubation produced truthful results.

In rebutting Porphyry's criticisms, Iamblichus divided theurgy into two levels. Low level theurgy involved magic rituals and spells performed to control and manipulate natural forces, to enchant others, and to conjure up spirits to do the theurgist's bidding. High level theurgy was practised as an aid to self-transformation in order to obtain insights into the world, and eventually as a means of merging with the One. This higher level was Iamblichus' focus.

Regarding dreams, Iamblichus noted that while some dreams certainly offer sound solutions to life problems, many dreams are no more than projections of fear, desire and imagination. Iamblichus also observed that periods just before falling asleep and just after waking, when awareness is detached from the body and so is open to subtle communication, provide a useful opportunity for enquirers to gain answers to vexing questions. With respect to incubation practices used in the temples of Asclepius, Iamblichus made the point that due to centuries of diagnoses the Greeks now had a sound basis for offering medical treatment, based on case studies as much as on dream diagnosis.

Oracles were widely consulted across the Greek and Roman worlds, the most famous being the oracle at Delphi, which was actively consulted from around 1500 BCE until the sanctuary was shut down in 395 CE. To Porphyry's objection that oracles got high on gases or sacred water, Iamblichus responded that anyone could drink the sacred water at Colophon, yet only the oracles gave inspired guidance. Instead, he drew a distinction between preparation and possession. Oracles drank water, breathed fumes, fasted, and withdrew to solitary places as preparation, in order to achieve a state of heightened awareness. It was in that heightened state the god entered them. And it was the descended god—he left open what the god might be—who spoke the words votaries heard, not a stoned pretender.

On the other hand, Iamblichus agreed with Porphyry that some people certainly did pretend to have access to higher knowledge, making astute guesses and interpreting sacred symbols skilfully. As a result they gave the impression of possessing knowledge. However, instead of opening themselves up to god-sent inspiration, they relied on their own character. Some even embraced dark arts and evil daemons in order to persuade others that they knew what the others didn't.

For Iamblichus, a theurgist could only be certain that inspiration was true and from the gods as a result of living purely and not seeking personal power, status, or acclaim. As Iamblichus put it:

> Whoever are gods in the true sense, they alone are the givers of good things, and associate only with good men, and mingle with those purified by the sacred science. ... But as many as are themselves guilty of crime, they fall upon and assault the divine in a lawless and disorderly manner and are not able to attain to the gods. These, then, being full of passion and evil, draw evil spirits to themselves because of kinship. ... [But from the pure theurgists] every evil spirit retreats and is overthrown and they are filled from above with the fire of truth. ... This, then, is one kind of mantic, which is undefiled and sacerdotal, and truly divine. And it is proper for everyone who is a genuine lover of the gods to surrender himself to it wholly. For in such a fashion arises, at the same time, both infallible truth in oracles, and perfect virtue in souls.

Like ascetic mystics, theurgists had to prepare themselves psychologically, expunging negative attitudes and lower emotions, and studying the esoteric sciences in order to access heightened states of awareness and thereby interact with the immaterial realm.

To put this less formally: you don't just build an altar, swing a cape embroidered with magical symbols over your shoulders, light a few candles, set incense smoking, maybe smoke a little something yourself, mutter incantations, ask for the desired goodies, and voilà! ... that which you desire magically turns up.

Iamblichus saw this as child's play. What he sought was something much greater, more intoxicating, more magically mysterious. In doing so, he presented the mystic quest in terms suited to his era.

His culture was dominated by religious and magical thinking. People sought divine signs and guidance from the gods. So in his theurgic approach Iamblichus acknowledged this was the social and religious context, then constructed an approach so the normative magical outlook could be used to achieve something quite unforeseen by the average worshipper: a way to personally commune with the separate reality. This, beyond all the god language, is what beats at the heart of the ancient occult exploration of reality.

THE ALLURE OF THE OCCULT

Throughout history human beings have been drawn to the realm of experience nominally called the occult. Whether seeking signs hidden in the world around them, or exploring non-ordinary perceptions deep within their own psyche, our forebears' pursuit of the non-everyday via heightened states of awareness has taken many forms, from shamanistic vision quests, to pyramid rituals, to sitting on corpses, to meditating in forests, to crawling deep into pitch-black caves.

Introverted asceticism and extroverted occultism are just two of the many possible approaches people have adopted in order to open up their awareness to the separate reality. In this sense, ascetic and occult practices are sub-categories of mysticism. But they overlap in significant ways. Each requires the foundation of inner purification, each involves engagement with otherwise hidden inner subjective capacities, and each aims to transcend the everyday world and its associated everyday self to achieve deeper insights into reality—given that historical records indicate that ascetics regularly underwent occult experiences, while those exploring the occult drew on a foundation of asceticism. For example, both Jesus and the Buddha underwent the occult experience of being tempted by the Devil, who appeared during ascetic disciplines. And as Iamblichus made clear, occultists were required to give up their grasping personality, break self-limiting behaviours, and reorient their psychology, in order to engage with alternative reality.

Nonetheless, and this is despite Jesus' clearly performing occult feats (such as turning water into wine, causing a fig tree to wither, and undertaking a shamanic journey to the lower world in the period between his crucifixion and resurrection), occult practices have been almost universally condemned by Christian churches. This condemnation was blunted a little in fourteenth century Italy, when Marsilio Ficino, under the sponsorship of Florence's ruler Cosimo de Medici, brought the esoteric philosophies of the Hermeticists, Iamblichus, Plotinus, Plato, and Pythagoras back to life and smuggled occult notions into Christian intellectual circles. As described earlier, the result was that during the sixteenth century the esoteric occult philosophy was adopted across Europe by enthused researchers, writers and scholars. However, this interest was only sustained by a few among the educated. Everyone else, including most of the clergy, remained suspicious of occultism—given this was a time when the occult included mathematics and astronomy, and when navigation, chemistry and medicine joined alchemy and witchcraft on the list of disreputable activities.

In this context, seventeenth century Enlightenment thinkers initiated a necessary change in outlook when they split mathematics from the occult, science from superstition, and laid the foundations of the modern naturalistic world view. However, they also bundled up the occult with religious beliefs and thrust them both into the basement, along with mythology, esoteric philosophy, and all the other non-naturalistic approaches that they judged humanity no longer needed. In doing so, they intended that the irrational occult would be forgotten. It wasn't.

THE VICTORIAN OCCULT REVIVAL

During the Victorian era occultism underwent a revival. As described in Chapter Two, the occult was brought up out of the basement and given pride of place in the drawing room, where seances and palm and teacup readings were enthusiastically carried out. In effect, Victorian drawing rooms became laboratories into which participants willingly placed their own awareness as a crucial element in experiments involving human perception. At the same time, anthropologists, archaeologists, philologists and historians spread across the planet, investigating many varieties of occult activities, such as Japanese ancestor worship, Chinese Taoist magic, and African and Haitian Vodou.

Underpinning these investigations was a newly adopted non-judgmental scientific perspective. This approach didn't just uncouple occult activities from old religious prohibitions, it unshackled the occult from the gods completely. Just as those in the sciences sought to understand the world in purely physical terms, without drawing on ancient mythology or referring to gods plural or singular, so Victorian explorers of occult phenomena sought to understand non-ordinary abilities and states of awareness in psychological terms. It was no longer necessary to say, with Iamblichus, that the theurgist was possessed by a god. Instead it could be said that the occult explorer had tapped into abilities that were latent within his or her own consciousness.

The ritual practices of ancient theurgy were transformed into an extended series of investigations into psychospiritual phenomenon, and with it our sense of what constitutes magic was remodelled.

CHAPTER EIGHT

Magic and its Dissenters

WE EACH CRAVE at least a little magic in our life. Yet transforming magic is hard to find. So we settle for lesser replacements: a favourite food, a special holiday, even just a night out with the girls or boys. The search for magical days, hours or moments is an expression of a deep desire to escape the mundane and rise into heightened experiences. At such times we leap out of the straight-jacket of daily existence and, for a while at least, swoop and soar.

This is why we embrace the sciences, religions and art. They offer us thought-provoking, ecstatic, even transcendent insights. In their very different ways, the sciences, religions and arts offer us revelatory moments of magic. Our craving for the magical takes us to concert performances by favourite musicians, to galleries and museums to witness extraordinary artistic achievements, and to movies and books to escape to other worlds where we can go on amazing journeys with characters whose lives are touched by magic, and who sprinkle a little on ours.

Our desire for magical revelations takes us to talks by experts, to encounter groups, to meet priests, writers, clairvoyants and celebrities. Closer to home, families bloom from the magical act of two people falling in love. It is as if the urge to seek the magical, in all its myriad forms, is woven into our DNA.

BEING TRANSPORTED BY THE MAGICAL

One of the principal allures of religious gatherings, from the Greek Eleusinian Mysteries to the Catholic mass, is that they are designed to provide a magical experience. Imagine what kind of experience the mass furnished in the Middle Ages for believers, mostly illiterate and possessing little, who spent their lives toiling for demanding masters with no control over their existence. Then they entered a light-filled church containing dazzling statues and richly coloured stained glass windows, where they witnessed a religious ceremony performed by men wearing ornate robes, uttering the mysterious language of the Church (Latin), punctuated by transporting music. In the context of their lives, the mass must have been an elevating experience that offered not just an image of heaven, but also an intoxicating taste of the divine in the midst of humdrum daily existence.

The same likely occurred during the height of the classical music era, when people first heard the symphonies of Beethoven and the operas of Mozart and Verdi. The streets of European cities were dirty and hazards constantly threatened, whether the bite of a rabid dog, a drunkenly waved knife, or a chamber pot emptied overhead. During winter mud was everywhere, while in summer the city reeked, flies swarmed and, seasonally, plague struck. In contrast, in the concert chamber listeners were enveloped in intoxicating music and lifted out of it all. Today we are in severe audio-visual overload, so hearing a Beethoven symphony or a Chopin waltz is just another audio input. But in an era when people were not incessantly pounded by music, such concerts must have been magical, even spiritual, experiences.

All this applies to the sciences. The daily grind of scientific research is often tedious, as research programmes are planned and carried out, measurements meticulously made, data sifted and collated, reports written up, funding to continue the next phase of research sought, and the whole cycle is then repeated. However, behind this humdrum activity scientists are engaged in a quest just as intoxicating as those undertaken by artists and religious seekers. The scientific quest treats objective reality as a mystery, a riddle to be grappled with to extract profound understanding. This is reflected in the way physicist Stephen Hawking voiced the hope that mathematics will one day enable human beings to penetrate the mind of God. For Albert Einstein the scientific quest itself was fuelled by a mystic urge:

The finest emotion of which we are capable is the mystic emotion. Herein lies the germ of all art and all true science. Anyone to whom this feeling is alien, who is no longer capable of wonderment and lives in a state of fear, is a dead man. To know that what is impenetrable for us really exists and manifests itself as the highest wisdom and the most radiant beauty, whose gross forms alone are intelligible to our poor faculties—this knowledge, this feeling ... is the core of the true religious sentiment. In this sense, and in this sense alone, I rank myself among profoundly religious men.

The magical experience scientists seek is that ecstatic moment of revelation when, in a flash of insight, they illuminate a tiny part of the riddle that is reality and fly out of themselves, carried into the heights of understanding on the wings of their questing mind.

Yet complicating this scenario is that what was once considered an act of magic may today be just a normal aspect of human existence.

MAGIC IS A CHANGING COMMODITY

Magic, like mysticism, takes two basic forms. There is magic in the general sense of a magical, transporting experience, as I have just applied the word. Then there is magic in its technical sense, of carrying out acts that defy logic or apparent natural possibilities, events that have an extra-natural component, that even, as in the case of Jesus, magically cause a dead person to revive. This puts technical magic into the category of supernatural activity. But—and it's an interesting but—how we define supernatural acts changes from era to era.

Historically, one of the greatest acts of supernatural magic has been performing miracles. Only gods and those blessed by the gods were considered capable of performing miracles. Jesus, the son of God, miraculously turned water into wine, multiplied bread and fishes, and walked on water. The Catholic Church grants those who perform miracles the status of saints. Yet in today's world doctors regularly perform miracles. They reattach a hand, insert a new heart, alter a person's appearance, even bring the dead back to life. Does this make doctors agents of the supernatural? Are they saints? Or magicians? Even occultists? Clearly not. What was once magical is now just how we do things. Not only does this require us to constantly reevaluate what defines a magical act, it also means there is a problem with the long-standing categories of religiously approved magic, which includes miracles and sanctioned powers, and disapproved magic, which are usually categorised as supernatural and occult.

If a modern day doctor was transported back to the Middle Ages with all his equipment, and used that equipment to bring a dead person back to life, those present would be shocked. They would be convinced they had just witnessed a supernatural act. However, the witnesses would also assume that a dead person could only legitimately be brought back to life with God's help. If the doctor had not appealed to God in prayer during the "ritual" of reviving the dead patient, the witnesses would judge that he was engaged in diabolical arts, that he was collaborating with the Devil. So in response to the doctor's life-saving efforts, the medieval witnesses would likely have killed him.

The problem for those medieval witnesses was a lack of context. They would have struggled to understand what they were witnessing. Unfamiliar machines, white coats, face masks, rituals with no priest present, strange actions such as injections and cutting with electric saws (we're assuming the doctor took a generator with him)—it would all have been totally foreign. And because foreign, very scary. Faced by their fear, all the witnesses could do was fall back on what they knew, which was that Satan reigned in the realm of the scary. This meant the doctor was Satan's agent, for which he had to die.

This type of response is significant when we shift to evaluating mystical records and accounts of occult incidents. A problem arises that is similar to that experienced by the medieval witnesses. When something occurs that is outside our prior experiential range, that does not fit at all with what we know, how do we respond? Some would be intrigued by this new information. But most reject it, whether by claiming it is impossible, or condemning it for whatever reason makes sense to them at the time.

This rejecting behaviour is a manifestation of what is known psychologically as cognitive dissonance.

ACKNOWLEDGING COGNITIVE DISSONANCE

The psychological phenomenon of cognitive dissonance occurs when people attempt to maintain two or more contradictory concepts, values, or pieces of information at the same time ... and fail to do so. As a result they fall into a state of confusion.

This is not an unusual occurrence. Confusion often results when new information arrives that contradicts our long-standing beliefs or assumptions. This was the case in the hypothetical example of the modern day doctor plying his trade in the Middle Ages. A true life example is provided by the occasion when Paleolithic cave drawings were first discovered at Altamira, Spain, in 1880, by a farmer and his daughter.

When the eminent prehistorians of the day, led by Emile Cartailhac, first viewed the cave drawings they were flummoxed. Clearly, they were confronted with extraordinary artworks. Yet Cartailhac and his fellow experts had no doubt that Paleolithic peoples were far too primitive to create such exquisite art. In this instance there was a gap between the new data (the high quality drawings) and preexisting assumptions (ancient people were unsophisticated). Cartailhac and his fellow experts fell into a state of cognitive dissonance. When people experience a disconcerting emotional or mental state they seek to re-establish their prior equilibrium. Cartailhac did so by dismissing the evidence. He declared the drawings fakes created by a modern artist, and called the drawings' discoverers liars. By rejecting the drawings, Cartailhac's distressing cognitive dissonance passed and he re-established his previous equilibrium.

Yet a problem soon developed for Cartailhac. This was that more Paleolithic drawings were soon found in other caves in Spain and France. Cartailhac was wrong. He had privileged his desire to calm his cognitive dissonance over his scholastic duty to appraise without bias the evidence presented to him.

It could be said that Cartailhac's world view had been penetrated by a little unexpected magic. Today we certainly see Paleolithic cave art as magical. Indeed, that so much of it still exists is miraculous. But rather than be enchanted by what he saw, Cartailhac felt threatened. So he didn't embrace the magic, apply his professional skills to this new information, and rejoice that the world is more mysterious and contains many more riddles than any of us can imagine. Instead, he denied the riddle and eliminated the magic. He preferred what he already knew to the challenge that went with being enchanted.

It is beyond the scope of this book to examine all the reasons people reject on-the-ground reality in favour of what they want to believe. I have already considered how top-down religious assumptions historically clashed with bottom-up mystical experiences. Whether it takes twenty years, which is the time Cartailhac took to admit he was wrong (he did so on his deathbed), or whether it takes two thousand years (which is how long it took humanity to accept the view, first proposed by Greek thinkers, that the Earth orbits the Sun rather than the Sun the Earth), reality-on-the-ground will always eventually trump how-I'd-like-it-to-be or this-is-how-my-father/teacher/religion/profession-tells-me-it-is.

But to be open to data generated by reality-on-the-ground we need to be aware that cognitive dissonance is a psychological issue whenever new information is discovered. The process of automatically reverting to existing beliefs, assumptions, or professional explanations needs to be seen for what it is—an effort to defensively deal with cognitive dissonance by rejecting the new in favour of the known.

Openness is required if, at the start of the twenty-first century, we are to reconsider what the magical is constituted of and initiate a reevaluation of the human situation, and do so without bias, putting aside defensive posturing and abandoning outmoded twentieth century attitudes.

Life is a riddle, an enigma. In our quest to understand the world, to comprehend the nature and structure of reality, and to explore all the possibilities available to us within human existence, we find that each insight, each hard-won revelation, dusts us, little by little, with a beguiling sense that the world is full of the magical. And we wake each day to appreciate that we are living in the midst of an enchanting mystery. This openness to enchantment drives the mystical outlook.

I'll now consider how the mystic quest to unriddle life and embrace the transporting magical continues to manifest in the twenty-first century.

The Scope of New Mysticism

CHAPTER NINE

Bursting Reality's Boundaries

THE RUSSIAN ESOTERICIST P.D. Ouspensky sought an alternative reality that he proposed could be entered via the miraculous. For Ouspensky, the miraculous was a new road that helped the adventurous break through from their familiar world to an alternative realm, which Carlos Castaneda named a separate reality.

In premodern cultures, the miraculous was considered to manifest via magic and miracles. The wise were considered blessed and knowledgeable because they were magically connected to the separate reality, however that reality was conceived, which gave them extraordinary insight and powers: they could speak with spirits and angels, cure the ill, raise the dead, escape the limitations of the body, fly into the heavens, and see past and future with more than a mortal eye. Jesus, Buddha, Krishna, Zoroaster, Moses and Mohammed are examples of the greatest among the wise. For us they are extraordinary beings who exist far away, in the historical past, wrapped in the swirling mists of myths and legend. They continue to inspire because they accessed a realm many of us want to reach, whether we call it heaven, the magical, or the wellspring of human achievements, and whether we see ourselves as arriving there through inspiration, insight, grace, or by dint of sheer hard work.

Yet how can those who wish to explore the alternative, separate reality even begin their journey when, as Ouspensky observed, the new road that will take us towards it is the *miraculous*? The idea that we have to wrestle with something miraculous just to take our first step towards the alternative reality makes it a truly daunting prospect.

On the other hand, to adapt one of Lao Tzu's well-known sayings, a journey of a thousand miles begins from where our feet are now. So what we need to do is make the miraculous accessible. One way to do this is to view the miraculous itself in a new way. We can achieve that by thinking of the miraculous not as magical, but as anomalous.

THE ANOMALOUS AND NEW MYSTICISM

The anomalous is a deviation from the normal, the accepted, the known. In the context of mysticism, the anomalous includes any event, perception, or experience that provides us with a breakthrough from one layer of reality to another. In effect, the anomalous punches a hole in what we know and opens up what we do not.

Equating the miraculous to the anomalous in this way brings the miraculous much closer to us than we ordinarily think. When Paleolithic cave paintings were first discovered they were anomalies because their existence contradicted the assumption made by prehistorians that Paleolithic people were too primitive to create such accomplished artwork. A single anomaly can easily be dismissed. But when more Paleolithic cave paintings were discovered, the evidence mounted, and eventually the sheer numbers of anomalous cave paintings demolished the prehistorians' rationale for dismissing them. Paleolithic artwork then ceased being anomalous and was integrated into a redefined model of human prehistory.

Mysticism is currently undergoing the same kind of reevaluation. Instead of describing non-ordinary events as miracles or magical, and instead of dismissing them as false data, intrepid explorers are treating non-ordinary events as anomalies worth investigating further. By doing so they have opened up the new road that Ouspensky sought. I am identifying the explorers who walk this road as practising the new mysticism.

Commonly, what sets these explorers on the road is a profound experience of cognitive dissonance that cracks the agreed parameters of their world wide open.

THE NATURE OF AGREED REALITY

We live in agreed reality. Agreed reality is the world we are born into and raised in. It includes social norms, language, culture, styles of dress, food, and what we may or may not expect from life. Human beings successfully live together because we collectively accept the parameters of agreed reality. Even those who rebel against agreed reality do so in relation to the boundaries established by agreed reality.

Psychologically, agreed reality exists as a film or patina between us and the world. It is a lens through which we filter perceptions and within the bounds of which we respond to life around us. We assent to this lens because it enables us to participate. We are social beings. When we are born we naturally relate to our parents, family, and the wider community in which we are raised. By the time we are adults we have so aligned our perceptions and world view to the agreed reality in which we have been brought up that we have come to think of agreed reality as the *only* reality.

Of course, this isn't true. Culturally, human beings are raised in a variety of agreed realities. Travelling brings us face-to-face with this fact, exposing us to different norms, languages, cultures, dress and social expectations. Once we get over the cognitive dissonance this generates, we see that much of agreed reality is socially constructed, and further that agreed reality changes from generation to generation: attitudes seen as foundational to agreed reality for one generation may be abandoned by the next.

However, there is another level of agreed reality that is not in flux. This level maintains that as human beings we are each a socio-physical identity, possessing a body and a culturally conditioned personality. The details of socio-physical identity vary from culture to culture, but the psychological fact that we are raised to view ourselves as socio-physical identities does not vary. It provides the unchanging norm that underpins agreed reality for all human beings always: we are socio-physical identities.

Anomalies puncture this agreed reality. When travelling we can adjust relatively easily to slight differences in local agreed reality. But for those who have an anomalous experience that punctures their socio-physical identity, the impact is destabilising in the extreme.

WHEN AGREED REALITY IS PUNCTURED

Imagine you are, like Dante, walking through a dark forest. Many layers of branches hang over your head. You can feel leaf-covered ground under your feet. Further imagine this is not only how you have lived your entire life, it is also how everyone else you know has lived their life. So the forest is not just agreed reality, but the only reality ever experienced by you and everyone you know.

Then, one day, without knowing how you got there, you stumble into a clearing. For the first time you see the sky above your head and birds wheeling in the wind. At your feet is a cliff. Far below wends a foaming river. For the first time you observe distant mountains, and below them plains filled with herds of unknown animals. With a profound shock, you realise the forest is only a tiny portion of all that exists. Your view of reality is well and truly punctured!

Immediately, you want to tell everyone what you have experienced. But there is a basic problem with sharing punctured reality experiences. How do you describe them?

We are back at the problem of how do we share what we experience during the act of kissing? The fact that everyone has experienced a kiss gives us a context to discuss kissing. But how do you explain your experience in the clearing to people who have never entered a clearing, never seen mountains, never watched herds of wildlife teeming across a plain? Inevitably, you'll end up describing your experience using terms drawn from forest life. But forest terms don't adequately encompass what you experienced in the clearing. There is a gap between your experience and available language. Even more problematically, there is a gap between your experience and the experiences of those to whom you are trying to describe what you have experienced. Quite literally, they do not know what you are talking about.

An important category of records produced by those engaged in the new mysticism consists of the testimonies of people who have undergone an experience that punctured their notion of agreed reality. Subjective experiences are fundamental to being human. Testimonies of what people have experienced are fundamental to any evaluation of radically subjective, mystical states of awareness. But this raises an important question: how far can we rely on subjective testimonies?

This is an important question because in general scientists deal in hard data. Subjective experiencing has no place in the process of collecting scientific data. Scientists' subjectivity is excluded. Yet there is no way to objectively quantify what people undergo during punctured reality experiences. They hinge on what is subjectively experienced. That is their point. That they *are* subjective accounts enhances their value rather than diminishes it.

However, we also need to trust we are receiving reliable testimonies from people who have not misrepresented or exaggerated their accounts, and who are definitely not playing up to an audience. Accordingly, I offer three published accounts of punctured reality experiences that may be considered trustworthy. Two are by medical doctors, the third by a writer-journalist. In writing their accounts, each put their reputation on the line. Given all three are professionally trained to accurately observe and record, it is safe to accept that they have not misreported or unnecessarily embroidered their accounts. Simply, we can assume they are not lying.

PSYCHIC INSIGHT

The first testimony comes from Paul Brunton's *A Search in Secret India*. Having travelled to Mumbai in search of the same miraculous that Ouspensky identified, Brunton discovered that Mahmoud Bey, an Egyptian reputed to be a magician, was staying in the same hotel. Bey looked like "a handsome Frenchman, such as one might see any evening in the better restaurants of Paris". Yet Bey had such a sinister reputation that hotel guests broke off their conversations in mid-sentence and stared at him as he walked past. Intrigued, Brunton decided to ask Mahmoud Bey for an interview. What he got was an offer from Bey to show his abilities. Bey began by asking Brunton to think of a question.

My brain plays with a few thoughts. Finally, I write down a brief question. It is: "Where did I live four years ago?"

"Now fold the paper repeatedly until it forms a tiny square," he instructs me. "Let it be the smallest possible fold."

I obey him. Thereupon he draws his chair back to my table and faces me once again.

"Please clench the piece of paper, together with the pencil, in the palm of your right hand."

I hold the articles tightly clutched. The Egyptian closes his eyes. He appears to fall into a profound concentration.

Then the heavy lids open once more, the grey eyes look steadily at me, and he quietly says:

"The question which you asked—was it not, 'Where did I live four years ago?' "

"You are correct," I reply, astonished. This is a case of mind reading extraordinary!

"Now, please unfold the piece of paper in your hand," his voice breaks in.

I place the tiny scrap upon the surface of the table and slowly open out its many folds until the paper lies flat, extended to its original size.

"Examine it!" commands the other man. I do so and make a surprising discovery. For some unseen hand has written in pencil the name of the town where I lived four years ago. The answer has been placed immediately beneath the written question.

Mahmoud Bey smiles triumphantly. "There is the answer. Is it correct?" he demands.

I give a wondering assent, for I am baffled. The feat hardly seems credible.

Twice more Brunton asked Bey to repeat the experiment. Each had the same result, leaving him wondering about the nature of what he had witnessed.

Conjuring? I dismiss the suggestion as absurd. The paper and pencil were supplied from my own pockets, the questions were unpremeditated, while Mahmoud Bey has scrupulously put several feet between us at each writing. Moreover, the entire feat has been performed in the morning daylight.

Hypnotism? I have studied the subject and know well when any attempt at undue influence is being made. I know equally how to guard against it. And the mysteriously added words still remain on the paper. The facts cannot be gainsaid. He has read my mind (as I believe); he has somehow, by some inexplicable magic, caused certain words to be written by an invisible hand upon a piece of paper which I clutch tightly in my hand; and, finally, those words form correct replies to my question.

What is the strange process he uses?

As I ponder over the matter, I feel the presence of uncanny forces. To the normal mind, the thing is incredible. It is something alien and apart from sane existence. My heart almost stands still with a sense of eeriness.

When I first read this account it resonated with me not just because of what occurred spookily stepped outside agreed reality, but because I had experienced something similar. My mother had invited into our house a woman who foretold futures by reading palms. My mother wanted her to read my future, but she refused, saying she didn't like to do it for young people—I was only fifteen at the time. Instead, she asked me to ask a question mentally and she would answer it.

The question I asked was one I had been thinking about for some time. It was, should I choose to be a psychologist or a writer? The woman's answer was not at all what I expected. She said, pretty much in these words: "You should be a writer, because psychologists tend to go as nutty as their patients." The response was undoubtedly pragmatic, but it was the fact that she was able to read my mind so accurately—it wasn't a question I had discussed with anyone else—that I found truly disconcerting. Like Brunton, I could only wonder at what was involved.

DREAMING THE FUTURE

The second account was written by Dr Larry Dossey M.D. and published in his book *Reinventing Medicine*. Dossey was in his first year of medical practice when he had a dream that he said "shook my world". He dreamed he saw the four-year-old son of one of his medical colleagues shouting and struggling to take off a piece of electronic apparatus. Exasperated, the technician administering the test gave up and left the room. Dossey continues:

> I woke in the grey dawn with the sensation that the dream was the most vivid I had ever experienced—numinous, profound, "realer than real". In view of the dream's seemingly trivial content, I could not explain why I felt so deeply moved.
>
> It was time for me to go to the hospital. The morning was busy, and I forgot about the dream until midday. Then, while I was lunching in the staff area with Justin's father, his wife entered the room holding Justin in her arms. The boy was visibly upset, with ruffled hair and tears streaming down his face. Justin and his mom had come from the EEG laboratory, where the technician had just tried to perform a brain test on the youngster. Her record was flawless; never had she failed to obtain a quality recording—until she met Justin.
>
> By this time the dream was replaying itself in my mind, and I was stunned. I had dreamed the sequence of events in exact detail before they happened. Disturbed, I went to see Justin's father in his office. Could anyone else have known about these events? I asked. I wanted to know if someone could have leaked information to me that could have influenced my dream. Of course not, Justin's dad said; no one knew about the problem except the immediate family and the neurologist.
>
> Then I told my colleague about my dream. He realised in an instant that if my report was true, his orderly, predictable world had suddenly been rearranged. If one could know

the future before it happened, our understanding of physical reality was seriously threatened. He sensed my disturbance, and I sensed his. Our conversation dissipated into silence as we contemplated the implications of these events.

Within a week I dreamed two more times about events that occurred the next day, and that I could not possibly have known about ahead of time. Those three dreams were the extent of my "future dreams." I had not had such a dream before, nor have I had one since. It was as if the universe, having delivered a message, hung up the phone.

NOT DYING, FLYING

Dr Eben Alexander M.D. is a neurosurgeon who almost died when he contracted bacterial meningitis, which caused his body to shut down. He was in a coma for six days, during which time his neocortex stopped functioning. Effectively, he was braindead. Over several days his doctors gradually realised that there was no hope: the brain cannot cease functioning for so long and recover. They expected Alexander to die.

However, in this state Dr Alexander remained aware and went on a life-changing journey. His awareness travelled out of his body and initially entered a strange environment, a pulsing darkness, in which he felt constricted: "I was simply a lone point of awareness in a timeless red-brown sea." After a long period he began hearing exquisite music. At the same time a light approached. He slowly realised it wasn't a light but an opening.

The moment I understood this, I began to move up. Fast. There was a wooshing sound, and in a flash I went through the opening and found myself in a completely new world. The strangest, most beautiful world I had ever seen.

I was flying, passing over trees and fields, streams and waterfalls, and here and there, people. There were children, too, laughing and dancing. A beautiful, incredible dream world.

Except it wasn't a dream. This place I'd found myself in was completely real. I know my biology, and while I'm not a physicist, I'm no slouch at that, either. I know the difference between fantasy and reality, and I know that the experience I'm struggling to give you the vaguest, most completely un-satisfactory picture of, was the single most real experience of my life. In fact, the only competition for it in the reality compartment was what came next.

I was in a place of clouds. Higher than the clouds—im-measurably higher—flocks of transparent orbs, shimmering beings arced across the sky.

Birds? Angels? These words registered when I was writ-ing down my recollections. But neither of these words do justice to the beings themselves, which were quite simply different from anything I have known on this planet. They were more advanced. *Higher.*

When Eben Alexander finally woke and had recovered his previ-ous faculties and functioning—a recovery that astonished his doctors as much as the fact that he survived at all—he recorded his experi-ences while they were still fresh in his memory. He deliberately didn't read anything related to near death experiences (NDEs) so his memory wouldn't be tainted by others' accounts. What he underwent is re-corded in his best-selling book, *Proof of Heaven.*

The implications of Alexander's NDE are significant. Importantly, he realised that his neocortex was not functioning during his coma, yet not only had he been aware, his awareness had expanded and absorbed much more information than his everyday human mind was capable of. This so excited him he wanted to tell others about it.

I was wildly—and naively—eager to share these experiences, especially with my fellow doctors. What I'd undergone al-tered my long-held beliefs of what the brain is, what con-sciousness is, even what life itself means. Who wouldn't be anxious to hear of my discoveries?

Quite a few people, as it turned out. Most especially, people with medical degrees. They couldn't wrap their minds around what I was so desperately trying to share. But then, who could blame them? After all, I certainly wouldn't have understood it either—*before*.

I was the quintessential, good-natured, albeit sceptical doctor. And as such, I can tell you most sceptics aren't sceptics at all. To be truly sceptical, one must actually examine something, and take it seriously. And I, like many doctors, had never taken the time to explore NDEs. I had simply "known" they were impossible.

CHALLENGING AGREED REALITY

Such experiences contradict our notion of agreed reality. Psychologically, they lead to a state of cognitive dissonance. So what do we do with this striking new information that destabilises our outlook?

When trying to answer this question Eben Alexander realised that many people who claimed to be sceptics with regard to non-ordinary experiences were actually deniers. Real sceptics are agnostic. Sceptics do not automatically accept that there is anything significant in a punctured reality account, but they are willing to evaluate it even-handedly—assuming they are interested enough to do so. Deniers are not sceptical. Faced with information that generates cognitive dissonance, deniers refuse to accept that reality puncturing events actually occur.

We are back in the hallway, where laughter and whispers are audible behind closed doors. But those committed to a naturalistic outlook not only deny that whispers and laughter can be heard, they deny the room even exists. From the denier's perspective, none of what Dr Alexander said he experienced actually took place.

The central problem is experience—or rather, lack of it. What Eben Alexander experienced changed him from a denier who "knew" NDEs were impossible, to one who now appreciates they do occur. When we experience for ourselves what gives rise to whispers and laughter behind closed doors, we gain experiential knowledge. When we have an experience that in Larry Dossey's words "rocks our world" our appreciation of what is possible radically changes.

If, in a state of cognitive dissonance, we consider these three events are scarcely believable—which is an understandable response— the question becomes, how do we respond to our own cognitive dissonance? Do we process the implications of such experiences? Or do we ignore them, perhaps telling ourselves they never occurred?

The testimonies of Paul Brunton, Larry Dossey and Eben Alexander involve the experiences of psychic insight, precognition, and a near death experience. These accounts, along with my experience of mind-reading, record anomalous events that lie outside the bounds of agreed reality. If we consider the totality of all human experiences to be a field, then most of us are clustered around the centre of the field, our awareness focused on the everyday experiences that exist well within agreed reality. Anomalous phenomena break through the bounds of

THE STRUCTURE OF AGREED REALITY

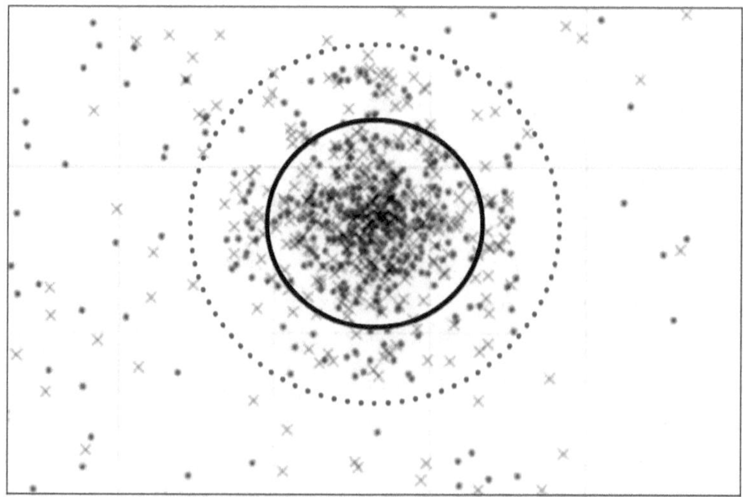

Agreed reality (experiences within the dark circle) is selected from the field of all human experiences. Accepting more experiences as valid expands agreed reality.

the everyday, offering us insights into aspects of reality that, while we call them alternative or separate, may more accurately be termed outlier experiences, occurring outside the normal human range.

Those involved in the new mysticism are driven by a desire to investigate outlier phenomena. This is why the enquiries at the heart of the new mysticism are so significant. Ultimately, they are contributing to a redefinition of what we consider constitutes agreed reality.

How are such explorations being carried out? Accounts suggest that for most people outlier experiences occur enigmatically and without warning. However, some inquisitive individuals, many with scientific training, have initiated research projects to explore outlier experiences in a more orderly way. I'll examine a selection of these studies next.

CHAPTER TEN

The Paranormal As Outlier

RESEARCHERS HAVE BEEN EXPLORING the paranormal for more than one hundred years, with a focus in recent decades on extrasensory perceptions, out-of-body experiences and near death experiences.

The first scientific investigation of paranormal phenomena occurred in 1831, when the French Academy of Science formed a subcommittee to review all available evidence of clairvoyance. Their task was to decide whether such experiences were faked by charlatans or whether clairvoyance could legitimately occur. The committee concluded that there was sufficient evidence supporting clairvoyance to warrant further investigation. However, the report was set aside and no one acted on the committee's recommendation. British scientists were the next to examine the paranormal.

PHANTASMS OF THE LIVING

In 1882 the British Society for Psychical Research was founded to investigate hypnosis, telepathy, ghosts, materialisations, and similar phenomena. The Society's members included scientists, clergy, university professors and members of Parliament. *Phantasms of the Living* (1886), written by three Society members, and approved for publication by the Society's council, is a thorough presentation of the Society's investigation into telepathy.

Two lines of research were undertaken. The first was an investigation of thought transference in laboratory conditions, in which the ability of one subject to transfer images, numbers and drawings to another's mind was measured. The second reviewed personal accounts of spontaneous telepathy, such as when a person far from a loved one knows of their illness or becomes aware of their death at the time it occurred. Methods were developed for reviewing data and for ensuring questionable data was excluded. The result was that sufficient evidence was found to confirm both forms of telepathy. The book-length report ends with a statement of hope:

> As the idea of Telepathy becomes understood, the difference will be more and more realised between facts which make for it and facts which do not. ... As for the merely negative difficulties—the general grounds of objection to our work—we see them already diminishing from the mere spirit of the age. The set of that spirit is very observably towards a wider tolerance—a distrust of finalities and restrictions, by whatever party imposed, and a faith in free inquiry, wherever it may lead.

Unfortunately, the authors' faith that people would pursue whatever free enquiry uncovered did not eventuate. Following the publication of *Phantasms of the Living*, scientific investigation of paranormal phenomena progressed stutteringly. In 1911 researchers in the United States universities of Stanford and Duke initiated projects to measure paranormal abilities in laboratory experiments. After being interrupted by WW1, these studies were taken up again in the 1930s. J.B. Rhine's book *New Frontiers of the Mind* (1937) presented the positive results of card-reading experiments undertaken at Duke University, but when follow-up attempts to repeat the experiments failed, manifestations of the paranormal were dismissed as imaginary and its investigation was derided as pseudo-science.

A significant step was taken when, at Rhine's instigation, the US Parapsychological Society was established in 1957. Its goal was to use scientific methods to investigate paranormal phenomena. According to the Parapsychological Society:

Parapsychology is the scientific and scholarly study of three kinds of unusual events (ESP, mind-matter interaction, and survival), which are associated with human experience. The existence of these phenomena suggest that the strict subjective/objective dichotomy proposed by the old paradigm may not be quite so clear-cut as once thought. Instead, these phenomena may be part of a spectrum of what is possible, with some events and experiences occasionally falling between purely subjective and purely objective. We call such phenomena "anomalous" because they are difficult to explain within current scientific models.

Most parapsychologists today expect that further research will eventually explain these anomalies in scientific terms, although it is not clear whether they can be fully understood without significant (some might say revolutionary) expansions of the current state of scientific knowledge. Other researchers take the stance that existing scientific models of perception and memory are adequate to explain some or all parapsychological phenomena.

Human knowledge progresses when a few visionary and brave explorers enter territory no one else is even sure exists, let alone is willing to investigate themselves—Christopher Columbus sailing west across the Atlantic, and being expected to fall off the edge of the world, is an example. When members of this intrepid advance guard return and report what they have discovered, others become intrigued, and more explorers follow. Over time, the static majority becomes comfortable with the new territory. Consequently, new boundaries of human knowledge are established.

In this chapter I will survey what four intrepid explorers have discovered in the field of the paranormal. But before doing so, I'll recount a study that raises a psychological issue that is not frequently discussed in relation to mysticism, but that is basic to all non-everyday experiences.

THE PAIN OF DOING NOTHING

In 2014, researchers discovered subjects would rather inflict pain on themselves than spend fifteen minutes in silent reverie. The research was undertaken in the Department of Psychology at the University of Virginia. Led by Erin C. Westgate, an experiment was initiated involving 55 university undergraduates, 31 female and 24 male, aged 18 to 25. The aim was to test the state of reverie and to examine how much people did or did not enjoy a situation in which they had minimal external stimulation. A paper was produced at the conclusion of the research: *The Pain of Doing Nothing: Preferring Negative Stimulation to Boredom.*

The experiment began with subjects being introduced to positive and negative stimuli. These were predominantly pictorial. However one negative stimulus involved a self-applied electric shock. The subjects were then placed in a room for between six and fifteen minutes. They had nothing to do but think. They were also offered the opportunity to shock themselves to pass the time if they wished.

The results were intriguing. Overall, participants did not enjoy mental reverie, reporting it was "difficult" and "boring". A substantial percentage of participants (67% of men, 25% of women) opted to voluntarily self-administer an electric shock rather than sit quietly with their thoughts. While the subjects in the above study were all from the "cellphone generation", and so might be expected to have difficulty focusing for p to fifteen minutes, Westgate found that older subjects experienced the same difficulty.

I had my own public experience of this discomfort when I attended a performance of music by composer John Cage. One piece was titled 4'33". It has no music. Instead the musicians sit silently at their instruments for the duration of the piece. The sounds the audience makes provides the performance. The concert I attended was held at the University of Auckland, so the audience was educated and all likely knew of the piece. Nonetheless, audience members were unable to cope with sitting in a state of reverie for four and a half minutes. As with Westgate's subjects, most needed external stimulus. In less than a minute whispers, chatter, then laughter, broke out.

Erin Westgate's comment on this behaviour is suggestive. She observed that perhaps thinking, and being comfortable doing so, is a learned skill for which training is required. She stated: "We don't expect everyone to get up tomorrow and run a marathon without extensive training. Maybe we shouldn't expect people to get up and think hard and seriously and enjoy it without the practice and experience of learning how to do that."

This leads to a fundamental question. What happens when people *do* learn to quieten and focus their thoughts? Even more pertinently, what happens when people learn to focus their awareness? As we saw in the survey of traditional mysticism, learning to focus both thinking and awareness is basic to mystical practices.

Much of the new mystical research into outlier abilities and experiences explores what happens when focus is achieved. The following example is from a study into extra-sensory perceptions.

THE GANZFELD EXPERIMENTS

Today extra-sensory perceptions are divided into three categories: clairvoyance, which involves perception of objects or events without using the body's senses; telepathy, which consists of direct communication between minds; and precognition, knowing about events that haven't yet occurred. ESP thus forms a subset of paranormal phenomena.

Those engaging in parapsychological experiments do not do so with hopes of forging widely respected scientific careers. An example is provided by the way deniers treated the research data gathered by Charles Honorton, an American parapsychologist who had extensive involvement in ESP experiments. Honorton originally worked with J.B. Rhine, who invented the term extra-sensory perception. He then went on to research at the Maimonides Dream Laboratory, where the parapsychological content of dreams was studied. Promising results were obtained from this research, however the Dream Lab proved too expensive to operate and was closed in 1978. Little work investigating the paranormal content of dreams has occurred since. Given the role dreams have played in mystical traditions throughout history, and that the Dream Laboratory's research showed that half of all psychic phenomena occur during dreams, this is clearly an area that requires renewed investigation.

After leaving the Maimonides Laboratory Honorton initiated a series of ganzfeld experiments. Ganzfeld is a German word that means "total field". The idea is that the subject is relaxed and seated in an undifferentiated perceptual field. In theory, the reduction of external stimuli facilitates the perception of paranormal phenomena. Honorton's previous research had shown that ESP effects are much weaker than impressions we receive via our senses. Honorton hypothesised that if he reduced standard sensory noise he would enhance subjects' receptivity to ESP. The aim was to generate data that either confirmed or denied the occurrence of ESP.

The experiment involved seating subjects in a comfortable chair situated in an acoustically sealed room. Headphones were placed over their ears, and their eyes were covered with the cut halves of a table tennis ball. A reddish light was turned on, which was perceived visually as a generalised red haze. After the subject had been sitting quietly for fifteen minutes, a sender in another room opened a sealed envelope and took out a card containing one image out of a possible four, or else viewed a randomly selected video clip, again one out of four. The sender then focused on the image or video and attempted to send it to the receiver in the next room. After thirty minutes the "sending" part of session was concluded. The receiver was then shown the four images and the four video clips and asked to rank them in order from 1 to 4. Only a ranking of 1 was considered a hit. If the sent image or video clip was ranked 2 to 4 by the receiver, it was labelled a miss.

In 1982 Honorton presented his results at the annual convention of the US Parapsychological Association. From forty-two ganzfeld studies carried out from 1974 to 1981, 55% percent of the studies showed statistically significant results. Many critics responded to the research, among them Ray Hyman. In a published meta-analysis of Honorton's data, Hyman suggested much of it could be discounted due to faulty methodology. Hyman concluded the result was actually close to 25%, that being chance. Honorton countered. He adjusted his own analysis of the data as suggested by Hyman, and still came up with a hit rate of 35%. The odds against this 35% hit rate occurring by chance was one billion to one. Hyman and Honorton then discussed the experiment. After working through various methodological issues, they then did something never done in the history of twentieth century ESP experiments: those having pro and anti positions on paranormal phenomena published a joint public statement:

> We agree that there is an overall significant effect in this database that cannot be explained by selective reporting or multiple analysis. We continue to differ over the degree to which the effect constitutes evidence for psi, but we agree that the final verdict awaits the outcome of future experiments conducted by a broader range of investigators and according to more stringent standards.

With Hyman agreeing that further experiments would be useful, he and Honorton worked together to define the more stringent standards. Honorton accepted all Hyman's demands. Honorton then began a second series of ganzfeld experiments using the stringent standards.

While Honorton was undertaking these experiments, the US Army employed the National Research Council (NRC) to review data its researchers had gathered during several years of studying the ways that paranormal abilities might be used to enhance intelligence gathering and human performance in battle. Techniques investigated included learning while asleep, telepathy, and clairvoyance. The NRC appointed a committee headed by John Swet. John Swet in turn brought in Ray Hyman to review the paranormal data.

The NRC's report was presented in December 1987. During the press conference to announce the report, John Swet stated: "The committee finds no scientific justification from research conducted over a period of one hundred and thirty years for the existence of parapsychological phenomena." In asserting this, Swet ignored the reports produced by the French Academy of Sciences and the British Society for Psychical Research, as well as other university studies such as those inittaed by Rhine. Ray Hyman not only agreed with Swet, he added that he was disappointed in the quality of the paranormal data produced. In saying this he deliberately ignored the data produced by Honorton, data he had earlier agreed indicated a "significant effect".

The denial of Honorton's work went further. During the preparation of the NRC's report, Robert Rosenthal, a psychologist from Harvard University, was asked to report on the quality of ESP research outside the Army's study. He agreed with Hyman that the overall quality of research was poor. However, he excepted Honorton's ganzfeld experiments, which he found met "the basic requirements of sound experimental design". He also agreed with Honorton that his results were well above chance, placing them at 33%, compared to Honorton's 35%. Rosenthal's report was not appreciated by Swet, who asked Rosenthal to withdraw the part of his report that supported Honorton's ganzfeld data. When Rosenthal refused, Swet excluded Rosenthal's conclusions on Honorton's data from the report.

Meanwhile, Honorton continued with his second set of ganzfeld experiments. These were carried out between 1982 and 1989, using Hyman's stringent methodology. Instead of four target stills and four target videos, the experiment now had eighty still images and eighty video clips. More video clips were included because the first set of studies had produced stronger responses when dynamic video was used.

The entire process was now automated, with a computer randomly selecting the still or video to be "sent" telepathically. Two stage magicians who specialised in faking ESP effects were brought in to ensure no cheating or deception occurred at any stage. They approved the experimental process. Over a period of six years and a total of 354 sessions, a hit rate of 34% was achieved, with one group consisting of 20 undergraduates from the Julliard School of Performing Arts achieving a hit rate of 50%.

Lack of funding led to Honorton discontinuing his autoganzfeld experiments in 1989. He died in 1996. However, by 1995 three more studies, at the Universities of Amsterdam and Edinburgh, and at North Carolina's Institute for Parapsychology, achieved hit rates of 37%, 33% and 33% respectively, when 25% would be expected by chance.

Multiple lines of possible future research arise from Honorton's data. What is the psychological mechanism by which ESP occurs? Is it the same mechanism for everyone, or are there varying mechanisms that suit different people? Is there a test for identifying ESP ability? Does everyone have the same potential for ESP? Can ESP abilities be learned? Are some people better senders and others better receivers? This is work for future researchers.

The whole field of parapsychological research remains contentious. Supporters claim multiple ESP effects have been validly recorded, while deniers refuse to accept that any significant effects have been recorded at all. What is lacking on the deniers' side is objectively applied science—very few deniers have carried out paranormal experiments themselves, and none approach data confirming ESP without preconceptions. What is lacking on the experimenters' side is systematic, extended explorations of all the possible varieties of parapsychological phenomena. As statistician and parapsychological researcher Jessica Utts observed in 1995: "The total human and financial resources devoted to parapsychology since 1882 is at best equivalent to the expenditures devoted to fewer than two months of research in conventional psychology in the United States." This lack provides an excellent opportunity to extend our knowledge of outlier psychic abilities, as well as to enlarge our understanding of what constitutes the full range of possible human perceptions of reality.

REMOTE VIEWING

The previous example was an objective experimental study, carried out by researchers on others. This next example presents a view from inside the ESP experience. Joseph McMoneagle is a specialist in remote viewing. Drawing on over thirty years of practice, McMoneagle defines remote viewing as "a human ability to produce information about a targeted object, person, place, or event, while being completely isolated from the target by space, time, and other forms of shielding."

A remote viewing protocol was originally developed by Dr Russell Targ and Dr Harold Puthoff at the Stanford Research Institute

(SRI) in the early 1970s. It involves placing the remote viewer in an enclosed room. A target is chosen and no one in the room with the viewer knows what the target is. This double-blind method ensures that whatever results are obtained can only be obtained via the mind of the viewer, not by the viewer deviously extracting information from those present or reading subtle body cues. The aim is for each targeting session to be a pure test of ESP abilities.

The experiments were initiated because the CIA and US military had long been aware of claims other countries were using ESP to gather intelligence. During WW2 the Germans were reported to have experimented with psychics, and during the subsequent Cold War the Russians began exploring ESP for intelligence gathering. The USA military felt that they needed to investigate such claims, otherwise, if ESP was effective, they would be left behind. The CIA then contracted Targ and Putoff at SRI to test for ESP abilities in randomly selected subjects.

A major issue was ensuring that research had stringent checks in place so the data produced could not be explained away as either no better than chance or as having been produced by deception. Accordingly, Dr Kenneth A. Kress was contracted to oversee SRI's ESP experiments. In a personal report, published in the CIA's internal magazine in 1977, Kress concluded: "Tantalising but incomplete data have been generated by CIA-sponsored research. These data show, among other things, that on occasion unexplained results of genuine intelligence significance occur."

Lt Frederick Atwater, a counter-intelligence officer, read Kress' report, and saw that ESP could be used for intelligence gathering. Noting Kress' recommendation that more research was needed, he drove a new project. This initiative grew, through several stages, into Project Stargate. Atwater began by re-engaging Targ and Puthoff at SRI to test a number of military personnel in order to identify those with a talent for remote viewing.

By 1977 Joseph McMoneagle had been serving in the military for seventeen years, mostly in signals intelligence. He was asked to join a dozen others in a series of tests conducted by SRI over a period of two weeks. The tests required the subjects to describe a randomly selected locale to which a person had been sent to stand. McMoneagle identified five of six locations, and was close on the sixth. He became Project Stargate's Remote Viewer #1.

It took many months for McMoneagle to improve the quality of his initial results. Despite a decade of experimentation by SRI, no one understood what was happening, how remote viewing occurred, and what physical and psychological conditions enhanced or hindered the process. McMoneagle discovered what worked best for him by trial and error. One significant training exercise took place after seven months. The target was identified via an overhead photograph of an aircraft hanger surrounded by parked planes. McMoneagle was asked to view whatever was inside the hanger. After meditating for twenty minutes to settle his mind, he started drawing what he saw. It turned out to be a prototype of the US Abrams XM-1 tank. This weapon was such a closely guarded secret that few people had ever seen it.

Successfully describing the Abrams tank—along with other positive results, such as identifying where an agent was with no information except a social security number—generated considerable interest within military and intelligence agencies. Many different offices soon began requesting targeting missions. The results of almost all these missions remain classified. One unclassified result involves when, in 1979, the US Embassy in Tehran was broken into and dozens of people were kidnapped. Six permanent and part-time viewers were immediately deployed to identify what condition the hostages were in and where they were being held. McMoneagle recounts:

> What they got was more than they expected. They got a separate location for hostages who weren't really hostages and a different embassy where they were being held (the Canadian Embassy, where they were being protected). They got descriptions of three individuals who were not in the original pack of pictures, and a description of a separate building where they were being held captive. ... The actual physical locations of each of the hostages was reported, specifically where they

were being held, and how they were being treated, to the point that when one of the hostages was released early because of medical reasons, and shown the information we had accumulated, he was enraged. In his mind, the only way we could possibly have had such accurate information would be to have someone inside the embassy with the hostages, all the time they were being held, and if that was the case then why were they still being held? He was not allowed to know.

Throughout the 1980s, Project Stargate's remote viewers were tasked with numerous missions for the CIA, National Security Council, Defense Intelligence Agency, and branches of the Department of Defense. On the downside, the viewers faced considerable ridicule from others in the military who feared ESP, didn't want to accept the results, or had their own professional reasons for denying the effectiveness of non-traditional forms of intelligence gathering. Project Stargate was closed down in 1995 amid public controversy regarding how much money had been spent and what the programme had achieved. Public debate continues regarding the programme's success or failure. McMoneagle notes that most of their results remain classified, so those who deny the programme's effectiveness lack data to make a judgement.

Following the closure of Project Stargate, McMoneagle resigned from the military and set up a business utilising his ESP skills. This has led to him successfully demonstrating his skills live on television. He has also offered his services free of charge to help find missing persons. On the basis of his experiences, McMoneagle has listed what worked for him as he sought to develop his abilities.

After observing how trainee remote viewers develop their skills, McMoneagle has concluded that whatever raw ability anyone demonstrates when initially tested will be improved through practice by 50%. This means that for those with little natural talent, practice will not have much impact. But for those with strong ESP ability, practice can extend their abilities significantly. For McMoneagle, successfully developing ESP abilities begins with settling into the right state of mind. He considers the attitude fostered within Zen meditation, in which no rewards are expected and nothing particular is sought, to provide the ideal mental approach. He observes: "One learns to be an empty vessel, within which ideas can form that are relevant to an unknown location, event, object, person, or concept. These ideas are not connected to any personal desires, wants, issues, beliefs, or structures that may already exist within us." Thereafter, McMoneagle identifies five qualities of mind to be foundational:

o Overcoming fear.
o Eliminating negative aspects of the ego.
o Not expecting to achieve perfection. (McMoneagle's results have a consistent success rate of 60% to 70%.)
o Being open to growing philosophically and spiritually.
o Always questioning, thinking critically, and maintaining a healthy scepticism.

McMoneagle's experience is that remote viewing skills are developed in the same way as any other skill. Remote viewers begin from a foundation of natural ability, and that ability is honed over an extended period. Self-reflection is required to review what has been experienced, to separate what pragmatically works from what does not, and to identify personal strengths and weaknesses. Mastery involves practical expertise backed by knowledge gained through reflection.

However, expertise extends beyond mere viewing of the target. McMoneagle found that he was eventually able to identify historical antecedents and likely future outcomes in relation to the target. In addition, occasionally he perceived manifestations that existed beyond the target. The kinds of manifestations he is referring to opens up an entirely new area of subjective experiencing, beyond the field defined by ESP. To explore this even more distant outlier area, I'll examine the out-of-body experiences of William Buhlman.

GOING OUT-OF-BODY

In his twenties William Buhlman was a confirmed materialist. He happily accepted that reality consisted of matter and that the sciences satisfactorily explained the universe. Then in June 1972 he had a reality-puncturing experience that turned his world on its head.

During a discussion on the possibility of life after death, Buhlman's neighbour recounted an experience of floating above his body. Intrigued, Buhlman read all he could about out-of-body experiences. At this time the term "out-of-body" (OOB) did not exist, the common term being astral projection. After finding a book describing how to induce astral projection, Buhlman tried it in bed each night. For three weeks nothing happened and he became convinced that he was right all along, and that accounts of out-of-body experiences were imagined or just intense dreams. Then:

> One night about eleven o'clock I drifted off to sleep during my out-of-body technique and began dreaming I was sitting at a round table with several people. They all seemed to be asking me questions related to my self-development and state of consciousness. At that moment in my dream I began to feel extremely dizzy, and a strange numbness, like from Novocain, began to spread through my body. Unable to keep my head up, I passed out, hitting my head on the table. Instantly I was awake, fully conscious, lying in bed facing the wall. I could hear an unusual buzzing and felt somehow different. Extending my arm, I reached for the wall in front of me. I stared in amazement as my hand actually entered the wall. I could feel the vibrational energy of it as if I was touching its very molecular structure. Only then did the overwhelming reality hit me: *My God, I'm not in my body.*
>
> Determined to stand, I began to move effortlessly to the foot of my bed, my mind racing with the reality of it all. Standing, I quickly touched my arms and legs, checking to see if I was solid, and to my surprise I was completely solid, completely real. But around me, the familiar physical objects of my room no longer appeared completely real or solid; instead, they now looked like three-dimensional mirages. Glancing down, I noticed a lump in my bed. Amazed, I could

see that it was the sleeping form of my physical body silently facing the wall.

As I focused my vision on the opposite side of the room, the wall seemed to fade slowly from view. In front of me I could see a wide, green field extending far from my room. Looking around, I noticed a figure silently watching me from about ten yards away. It was a tall man with dark hair, a beard, and a purple robe. Startled by his presence, I became frightened and instantly "snapped back" into my physical body. Excited, I sat up, my mind exploding with the realisation of what had just occurred. I knew it was absolutely real, not a dream or my imagination. My entire ego awareness had been present.

This experience forced Buhlman to restructure both his idea of reality and his assumptions about personal identity. After this first revelatory out-of-body experience, he practised assiduously. He also kept records of his experiences. Buhlman eventually realised he was "waking up" in his energy body. This energy body was very close in size and shape to his physical body. And the energy world it occupied was also similar to his everyday physical world, with the bedroom in which he slept echoed in the parallel energetic realm. When he woke in his energy body he saw his physical body sleeping because the energy world overlaid the physical world. When his arm went through the bedroom wall during his first OOB experience, it was the arm of his energetic body that penetrated the wall of his physical bedroom.

By experimenting, Buhlman found the trick to moving energetically was to intend a movement in thought. It then occurred. Over time he learned to rise energetically out of his bedroom, hover over the house, and then fly across the neighbourhood, the city, and other places and landscapes. Occasionally, just as had happened to Joseph McMoneagle, Buhlman met other beings.

In a journal entry from 5 December, 1986, Buhlman recorded meeting the same being he had observed during his very first OOB experience. The encounter began with Buhlman not seeing anyone but being aware someone was near.

Out of curiosity I call out, "Who are you?" Images stream in my mind. "I'm an old friend who is observing your progress."

The feelings instilled in the images are warm and friendly. I'm completely at ease and firmly make a request: "I want to see you." I watch in amazement as the hazy outline of an image appears. A transparent hologram of a man becomes increasingly dense before me. He has dark hair and a short beard and wears a purple robe. At first I'm surprised by the reality of his rapid materialisation, but he seems to sense my discomfort and a series of comforting images appears in my mind: "No need to fear. You and I are old friends." I somehow sense his friendship and calm down.

Just like McMoneagle, Buhlman discovered that overcoming fear is key. Fear closes down the awareness so it cannot access the subtleties involved in paranormal experiences. On other occasions, when Buhlman was shocked or reacted fearfully, his awareness instantly returned to his physical body. On this occasion, having overcome his initial fearful reaction, he was given an insight into the equivalence between those dwelling in the human world and beings occupying the energetic realm.

As I stare at this man, he seems pleased to see me. He seems to know my thoughts and responds to the questions that fill my mind. "I'm just as you. The only difference is I don't possess a physical vehicle. ... I'm acting as one of your guides. You have different individuals assisting you in different aspects of your life. In a way, each person assisting you is a specialist in a given area of existence. You and I love to explore inward, so I am here to assist in that part of your life.

"Each person who has an out-of-body or near death experience has a guide present during the experience. Assistance is always available but must be requested. There is nothing to fear, but many are still unaware that their thoughts manifest their reality. ... As you are learning, thought control and focus are absolutely essential. This is especially true as you explore deeper within the interior of the universe. Your control is getting better, but you still have fears to overcome."

This offers an insight into the finer structure of reality that Mc-Moneagle referred to in his description of the fourth level black belt stage. In this variety of paranormal experiences deeper energetic levels of reality may be entered. It is then discovered that these levels are not empty but are occupied by other beings. This is what Alexander Eben found during his near death experience and that William Buhlman learned over the course of decades of OOBs. Buhlman's experiences have led him to conclude that far from physical reality being the only reality, physical matter may be considered to be a crust under which lies a vast realm of immaterial reality.

An unquenchable desire for knowledge is propelling a select number of explorers beyond the security of their physical homelands. These resourceful adventurers are exploring and charting the universe beyond the dense, outer crust of matter. This exploration and charting of our unseen energy-universe is of worldwide importance. ... The time has come for us to explore and discover the truth of our existence—to break free from the conclusions and assumptions of others, to see and know for ourselves.

William Buhlman's realisation that we can generate a crack in the crust of reality, through which awareness can travel to obtain non-ordinary knowledge, is far from new. It is basic to the shamanic world view.

MEETING MESCALITO

Learning to crack the fixed informational matrix generated by the body's perceptual system is central to every shaman's education. The trick is to sustain the perceptual break long enough for meaningful perceptions to occur. Anyone can "click out" for a few moments. Few are able to do so for minutes at a time, let alone sustain heightened states for hours.

Shamans have developed a number of techniques for doing so. Drumming, chanting, and dancing are central to facilitating heightened states of awareness. Fasting and illness can also bring on such states. Whatever technique is used, the shaman's purpose is to disrupt the stolid momentum of everyday awareness and open a perceptual crack in the world. However, to sustain a journey into the world beyond the crack requires energy. A lot of energy.

Methods for developing one's energetic resources include practising ascetic disciplines, engaging in theurgic exercises, developing paranormal abilities, and meditating. Another is to raise one's personal energetic state by learning, as Buhlman did, to shift awareness into the energetic body. But these methods take much time and effort. For shamans just beginning their quest, an age-old method for cracking the hard perceptual crust of reality has involved ingesting or smoking power plants. The psychoactive chemicals in power plants interrupt the brain's normal perceptual patterns and induce altered states of awareness.

During the 1970s, when I was at university, the most widely known accounts of what power plants did to the human psyche were in the books of Carlos Castaneda. Don Juan, Castaneda's teacher, introduced him to datura, mushrooms, and peyote on the grounds that they stimulated the expanded awareness necessary to obtain a view of the "separate reality". Castaneda's strangest experience occurred when he chewed buttons of the peyote cactus and met an identity Don Juan called Mescalito. On one occasion, during a four day mitote when he repeatedly chewed peyote, Castaneda felt he was being carried on black water. The water abruptly receded and he was left on the dry earth.

The place where I stood was a corral formed by enormous boulders. From among them came the most exquisite music. It was a fluid, uninterrupted, eerie flow of sounds.

At the foot of one boulder I saw a man sitting on the ground, his face turned almost in profile. I approached him until I was perhaps ten feet away; then he turned his head and looked at me. I stopped—his eyes were the water I had just seen! They had the same enormous volume, the same sparkling gold and black. I felt he was deliberately pressing on my chest with the pressure of his eyes. I was choking. I lost my balance and fell to the ground. His eyes turned away. I heard him talking to me. At first his voice sounded like the soft rustle of a soft breeze. Then I heard it as music—as a melody of voices—and I "knew" it was saying, "What do you want?"

I knelt before him and talked about my life, then wept. He looked at me again. I felt his eyes pulling me away, and I thought that moment would be the moment of my death. He signalled me to come closer. I vacillated for a moment before I took a step forward. As I came closer he turned his eyes away from me and showed me the back of his hand. The melody said, "Look!" There was a round hole in the middle of his hand. I looked into the hole and saw myself. I was very old and feeble and was running stooped over, with bright sparks flying all around me. Then two of the sparks hit me in the head and one in the left shoulder. My figure, in the hole, stood up for a moment until it was fully vertical, and then disappeared together with the hole.

He turned his eyes away and hopped like a cricket for perhaps fifty yards. He hopped again and again, and was gone.

Not unexpectedly, Castaneda found it difficult to comprehend what he had experienced. Complicating the situation was that he couldn't remember what question he had asked, and so was unable to interpret his vision. He also found the experience of altered states in themselves very difficult to reconcile with his Western world view. Driven by academic assumptions, Castaneda doubted that his experiences had occurred. Nor could he find a way to independently verify what he experienced, given that the only explanations he received were offered by Don Juan who had initiated the experience in the first place.

At issue is the polarity that is central to any appraisal of nonordinary phenomena: separating from an experience in order to appraise it objectively, while remaining subjectively connected to that experience. The first enables us to learn *about* an experience, the second helps us learn *from* an experience. While his reality puncturing experiences were challenging, it was the shift from detached observer to immersed participant that Castaneda particularly struggled with. "The belief system I wanted to study swallowed me. I am now faced with the special problem of having to explain what it is I am doing. I am very far away from my point of origin as an ordinary Western man or as an anthropologist, and I must first of all reiterate that this is not a work of fiction. What I am describing is alien to us; therefore, it seems unreal."

Critics contend that despite his denials Castaneda didn't actually experience what he claimed and that much of what he wrote *is* unreal. Nonetheless, his work raises fascinating questions. A central issue, not addressed by Castaneda's critics, is how can we validate anyone's nonordinary experiences when they are, by definition, alien to our notion of agreed reality and therefore, from our perspective, must necessarily be unreal, bizarre, and bordering on the unbelievable?

One response is to weigh one person's testimony against what others have experienced. An interesting comparison arises with William Buhlman, given he and Castaneda each met a non-physical identity who gave them pertinent life lessons. Islam has a tradition of Khidr, a supernatural being who taught Moses and has appeared to many people over the centuries. The notion of angels and saints who help those who ask is widespread throughout all religions. Cultural differences can be expected in the ways such identities manifest. For Buhlman the guide appeared as a friend, while for Castaneda it was as Mescalito, a peyote being. In India guides appear in the form of gods or sages. What this means is that the notion of spiritual guides has multiple affirmations across cultures and over time. Accordingly, Castaneda's experience of a non-physical guide cannot be automatically dismissed as fiction. Numerous people have had a related experience.

Another of Castaneda's experiences illuminates what Buhlman underwent. When sitting one day on a bench in a town square, Castaneda saw the passing people in the form of luminous eggs: "All at once the people in front of me changed into very large blobs of white light. Don Juan had told me that human beings appear to the seer as luminous eggs. They were big, in fact they were enormous, perhaps seven feet high and four feet wide or even larger."

Don Juan contended that on the energetic level every human being is a luminous egg, a cocoon, consisting of a bundle of energetic emanations. Everything else in the world also possesses energetic emanations. Perception occurs when energetic bundles from inside and outside the luminous egg are brought into alignment. Alignment occurs at the assemblage point on the luminous egg. Don Juan called the assemblage point for perceptions of the everyday world the first attention. When sorcerers crack the fixed crust of everyday perception, they shift their assemblage point to an alternative position on the luminous egg. Don Juan called this point the second attention.

> The new seers call the emphasised emanations on the right side, normal awareness, the tonal, this world, the known, the first attention. The average man calls it reality, rationality, common sense. These emphasised emanations compose a large portion of man's awareness, but are actually a very small piece of the total spectrum of emanations present inside the cocoon of man.
>
> The disregarded emanations within man's band are thought of as a sort of preamble to the unknown, the unknown proper consisting of the bulk of emanations which are not part of the human band and which are never emphasised. Seers call them the lefthand awareness, the nagual, the other world, the unknown, the second attention.

When the assemblage point shifts to the second attention, non-ordinary perceptions occur. Once a seer learns how to deliberately shift awareness into the second attention, awareness becomes pliable and is able to assemble all kinds of perceptions. One of these is the perception of the dreaming body, also called the double. It is called this because it is easy for the second attention to assemble an energetic replica of the physical body. Here Castaneda's account illuminates Buhlman's.

Buhlman observed that during his OOBs, when his awareness travelled to different realms, he acquired a different energy body that was energetically aligned with the domain to which he had travelled. In Don Juan's terms, what Buhlman did was shift the assemblage point of his awareness into the second attention, where he assembled the energy body that he initially used to fly through the skies above his house, then to visit distance places. Don Juan's explanation, that bundles of energetic emanations need to come into alignment for perception to occur, agrees with what Buhlman came to understand of his out-of-body experiences.

The point of all mystic disciplines, no matter what form they take, is to move awareness beyond the limits defined by agreed reality. Joseph McMoneagle's non-local perceptions, William Buhlman's experiences of different energy bodies, Eben Alexander's near death experience, and Castaneda's altered states of awareness, whether achieved as a result of applied disciplines, by taking psychoactive drugs, or by nearly dying, each serve the same purpose: shaking people out of their fixed body-centred perceptual matrix, cracking the rigid crust of their perceptions, and lifting them into an alternative perception of reality.

THE NEW MYSTICS

There is no doubt that paranormal phenomena remain troubling. Despite Victorian investigators unshackling the paranormal from the occult, and despite the authors of *Phantasms of the Living* anticipating an increased acceptance of outlier psychological phenomena, most people still regard the paranormal with uncertainty, trepidation, even fear. Their unease is understandable.

We are social creatures. By working collectively within an agreed concept of reality we make the best of our existence together. The paranormal challenges our assumptions regarding how human reality functions. Even more disturbingly, the paranormal challenges our sense of identity—because if McMoneagle did perceive kidnapped people in rooms half a world away, or if, in a state of full awareness, Buhlman really did rise out of his body, look down on it, and fly across the city, and if Castaneda actually communicated with a non-human identity, then these experiences radically challenge our ideas of what human beings are capable of and, correspondingly, what human identity consists of.

The naturalistic view of human identity is that we are a body and our mind is an epiphenomenon of our body. When our body dies, our brain dies, and our mind, awareness and identity die with it. But if our identity is not limited to our body, if in fact we are free-floating identities, then agreed ideas about human identity have to be completely rethought. If McMoneagle, Buhlman and Castaneda experienced only ten percent of what they describe, then as far as agreed reality is concerned all bets are off. A new collective agreement of what constitutes reality is required, and of human identity within it.

For individuals, establishing new notions of reality and of personal identity begins with a punctured reality experience. In effect, punctured reality experiences provide an initiation into a new way of looking at life, into a realisation that the universe is not structured the way that human beings collectively agree. Punctured reality experiences suggest there is something more going on, that a currently unknown level to reality exists, and that we possess an equally unknown capacity to access that hidden level of reality. There are three basic responses to reality-puncturing experiences.

One can turn one's back on them, ignore them, pretend they never occurred, and carry on as before. This is the denier's position.

The second response is to acknowledge that one has experienced something that is not part of the everyday, being open to the possibility of having a similar perception again, but not actively pursue that kind of perception. Often such events are thought of as being caused by an external agency, such as a saint, an angel, a deceased relative, perhaps even God, or are described as just "one of those things". In this response people acknowledge that punctured reality experiences occur, then carry on as before.

The third response is to actively explore the consequences of punctured reality experiences and of altered states of awareness. This naturally leads to questioning one's notions of reality and personal identity. It also leads to seeking more similar experiences in order to answer the questions that naturally result. Few people respond in this way, but those who do are mystics. In the terms being used here, those who additionally adopt an empirical approach, process their experiences without recourse to religious myths or metaphysics, and who describe their experiences in bottom-up contemporary terms, are participating in the new mysticism.

Today it is possible to enter the territory traditionally called mystical and occult with an open mindset, using a psychological and phenomenological approach. The fact is, the more we investigate the mystical, the more a conducive mindset becomes crucial.

IT'S ALL IN THE MIND

My earlier survey of traditional mysticism revealed that tuning one's psychological makeup has long been seen as fundamental to preparing for mystical experiences. The same applies to the new mystics.

McMoneagle, Buhlman and Castaneda all discovered that fear has to be overcome in order to explore outlier paranormal experiences. The fear comes from that part of our psychological identity that clings to the established, the fixed, the familiar. Everyone who explores the paranormal initially feels fear, because they are challenging their own fixed sense of self identity. The fear is likely to be followed by a period of cognitive dissonance. But any experience that is repeated becomes familiar. Repetition and familiarity lead to experiences being absorbed psychologically so they are no longer disturbing. The outlier is normalised. Part of normalisation involves accepting the previously abnormal as normal. Psychologically, the previously fixed sense of self is expanded to accommodate the new experiences.

The other point McMoneagle, Buhlman and Castaneda raise is the need for an open mind. A closed mind is a defence mechanism, a means for keeping anomalies at bay. Punctured reality experiences poke a hole in the fabric of the fixed and initiate a radical change in perspective. The English word metanoia refers to this type of change.

It comes from the Greek *metanoein*, which means change of mind. Becoming open to new perspectives and embracing new ideas, new emotions, new experiences and, ultimately, a new sense of personal identity, begins with a change of mind. If we do not change our mind, if we fixedly cling to what we have long believed, assumed, or "know", it is impossible to experience anything new. We shut it out.

In daily life our outlook is dominated by culturally conditioned ideas and attitudes we sustain within our everyday mind. Our everyday mind doesn't just keep us plugged into agreed reality: it is programmed by and totally grounded in agreed reality. But what if our everyday mind actually constituted only one part of our overall awareness? And what if, as the previous accounts suggest, our awareness is capable of extending itself beyond the limits imposed on and by our everyday mind, thereby enabling us to access alternative perceptions of reality?

William Buhlman likens material reality to a hard crust. Beneath the crust are vast regions of immaterial reality. Cracking the crust gives us access to those regions. Extending Buhlman's metaphor, it could be said that our everyday mind is a material crust laid over our awareness. Our crusty mind keeps telling us what it thinks is real and so keeps us grounded in agreed reality. But if we crack the crust, if we "change our mind", we open ourselves up to deeper perceptions. This is what punctured reality experiences do: they crack fixed notions, and new perceptions never previously imagined by the crusty mind flood in. To relate this to metanoia, I'll return to the metaphor of the forest.

METANOIA AS GATEWAY

Imagine that our existence is lived wholly under trees. However, in one part of the forest is the entrance to a cave. This cave is widely viewed as a dark and scary place. Sometimes strange sounds echo inside. For those living in the forest, agreed reality states that the cave is dark and dangerous, it is occupied by deadly creatures, and for their safety all need to stay well away.

But other stories are also told of the cave. There are tales that people once found precious jewels deep inside, that they discovered the cave links to other caverns, that there is actually a vast subterranean world, full of mysteries and wonders. These tales of wonder counterbalance the stories that sustain the forest peoples' fear. Nonetheless, no one is game to enter the cave to find out which stories are true and which are false.

Why not? Why do the forest dwellers live for generation after generation, walking past the cave, knowing it is there, but never going in? What is keeping them out? Only one thing: their own mind. The forest dwellers' minds, filled with tales of terrors and horrors, stop them from entering. This means that entering the cave depends on just one precondition: metanoia, a change of mind.

Punctured reality experiences may be likened to someone hearing wonderful music emanating from within the cave. Or seeing a dead family member at the entrance of the cave, waving them to come on in. Or having a dream in which it is felt that the cave is not dangerous, that exploring the cave promises instead a remarkable adventure. Punctured reality experiences break down our fixed ideas about the cave and offer us an alternative view of what the cave promises.

Of course, the cave is our own awareness. Paranormal experiences affirm that human awareness embraces a great deal more than we allow ourselves to consider, let alone experience. Our everyday mind stands outside the cave, its knees knocking. But our awareness is capable of jumping the fence of agreed reality and entering the unimaginable.

This is what the advance guard among scientists, religious believers and artists do: motivated to extend human knowledge, they push past the boundaries of the known and penetrate the unknown. The mystic journey is of the same order. The only difference is that the mystic doesn't journey into the vast world external to us but instead travels deep within, into the cavernous world that has just one guardian keeping us out: our own mind.

I'll now consider what contemporary bottom-up experiences can tell us about "entering the cave".

CHAPTER ELEVEN

Talking to Ghosts

IN HIS PIONEERING STUDY of shamanism, Mircea Eliade defined shamanism not as a doctrine but as involving techniques to induce an ecstatic trance state, in which the shaman journeys beyond the body to diagnose illness, find and facilitate cures, obtain solutions for people's life problems, view past or distant events, foresee coming events, contact ancestors, and aid the newly dead as they negotiate their entry into the afterlife. Spirit allies and guides are an essential contributor to what they learn and do.

To put this last statement into context, if we possess a spiritual awareness that exists in parallel to our body and its everyday social identity, and if this awareness has the ability to reach out beyond the mind of our everyday self, what aspects of reality does it access? Possessing ESP abilities so that distant people or events can be known is fascinating, but it is a passive state, given it involves observing but not actively engaging. The question is, besides the guides reported by Alexander in his near death experience, by Buhlman in his out-of-body experience, and by Castaneda in his peyote experiences, *who* or *what else* may we actively and consciously engage and interact with when we are in heightened states of awareness?

This is a question that fascinated the Victorian occult investigators. They wanted to know what spirit beings had to say about the connection between the human world and the spirit world. This is why the Victorians took part in seances and theurgic rituals, and investigated psychic abilities, mediumship, channelling, and dreams. They sought out non-everyday communication with non-physical beings, the type of communication that occurs regularly among shamans who obtain much of their knowledge directly from spirits. In this chapter I will consider what happens when we enter the cave of our awareness. Besides our own deeper self, what or who do we find there? Are such experiences useful? Or are religious prohibitions correct and "that way madness goes"? Most importantly, what can such experiences tell us about our own innate abilities and identity?

I'll begin by recounting a contemporary shaman's account of what he experienced when, in search of spirit knowledge, he spent a night in an actual cave.

HOOVES IN THE DARKNESS

Anthropologist Michael Harner is a leading authority on shamanic practices. Since the late 1950s, he has studied with shamans in Ecuador, Peru, North America, and Lapland. In 1987 he left academia to establish the Foundation for Shamanic Studies, an organisation dedicated to preserving, studying, and disseminating shamanic knowledge. Since then he has continued to study and learn with tribal shamans around the world. He is also strongly motivated to pass on what he has learned to others.

In 1982 Harner decided to carry out a power quest. It involved spending a night in a cave. His aim was to seek a special shamanic healing power that would enable him to better help others. Having found a suitable cave in Shenandoah Valley, Virginia, in the early evening light he paused at the entrance, said a prayer asking for assistance in his quest, then walked for fifteen minutes, penetrating deep into the cave. The procedure involved remaining in total darkness, sleeping until midnight, waking, eating, then staying awake for the rest of his quest. He wasn't to leave the cave until after dawn. After settling down to sleep, he became concerned he wouldn't wake in time. Then:

> I was shocked awake by a feathered wing gently brushing
> my face. I felt an adrenaline rush of excitement. I pressed
> the button on my wristwatch. The faint numbers showed

the time was two minutes before twelve. My astonishment at being awakened by the winged caress was accompanied by relief at being roused from my sleep. I groped for the sandwich, found it, and ate. [An hour of waiting followed.]

Suddenly, from the direction of the distant entrance of the cavern, came the sound of hooves. The sound became louder; it was clearly a herd of animals. I could not believe what I was hearing. The noise of their galloping got closer and closer. This seemed impossible. Yet the sound became so great I had to cover my ears. Was I to be trampled to death? I crouched down. Then the thundering hooves swept past on both sides of me, rushing deeper into the cave and beyond. Although I could not see them, I heard them snorting as they galloped by. "We are Horse," they said, in a communication like telepathy, but stronger.

Then another, smaller herd followed fast upon them, their breathing and hoofbeats not quite as loud. "We are Bison," they said. Then they were gone. The cave was silent again. I was ecstatic, truly ecstatic. Tears of joy and thanksgiving were running down my cheeks. It was a miracle. This was no dream, for I was still wide awake.

Then, as I was sitting there, an immense, indescribable power rushed toward me from the same direction that the herds had come. But this time there was no sound, no warning. It swept overwhelmingly through me like a freight train. A surge of immense energy filled my body. I was astonished. The power had come! Then the animal was gone. As it bounded soundlessly away through the darkness beyond the recesses of the cave, it called back to me: "I am XXX, XXX, XXX!" It said, "I am one and all. You and I are one." Then there was only silence. I felt indescribable awe and gratitude.

Shamanic protocol forbids Harner from naming his helping healing animal spirit. In part this reflects the shaman's desire to retain a respectful relationship with the spirit and to function as a clear conduit of the spirit's power. In this particular case, Harner sought to establish a connection with the spirit to facilitate healing. He provides an example of this working relationship when he was personally on the receiving end of shamanic spirit healing.

In the early 1990s, three eye specialists diagnosed Harner as having an incurable degenerative eye disease. Eventually, he would lose his sight. After hearing about the diagnosis, and that Harner and his wife would soon be holidaying in Hawaii, one of Harner's students suggested he visit Lanakila Brandt, a Hawaiian shaman-priest of part German descent, who was known for his healing powers. Harner arranged to meet the shaman and underwent treatment on five consecutive days. When he returned to the eye specialist all symptoms had disappeared. This so confused the specialist that he suggested the original diagnosis must have been wrong. It wasn't. What occurred was an impossible spirit intervention—impossible, that is, in terms of an agreed reality in which spirit interventions do not occur and incurable conditions do not suddenly vanish.

In many tribal cultures it is not just shamans but tribe members who regularly perceive and interact with spirits. These spirits fall into the categories of the spirits of ancestors, the spirits of plants, and the spirits of animals. Spirits are not equal. Each possesses particular powers, and some are more powerful or more knowledgeable than others.

Those living in traditional tribal cultures see the spirit world as directly connected to everyday human existence. Everyday reality and shamanic reality overlap, with causal relationships going both ways. In the case of Michael Harner's eyes being cured, a spirit affected the physical world. But it is also possible for those in the physical world to affect the spirit world.

GHOSTS OF THE TSUNAMI

On 11 March 2011, an undersea earthquake struck northern Japan. Centred seventy kilometres off the Oshika Peninsula, it was so powerful it shifted the Earth on its axis. It also generated a devastating tsunami. Over a million buildings were damaged. Entire towns were obliterated.

In an instant, families were broken and homes and occupations vanished. Life for well over 300,000 people was irrevocably changed.

Understandably, the survivors were traumatised. In the aftermath of the disaster, traditional forms of burial were not possible. The Japanese normally cremate their dead. However, the crematoriums could not cope with the numbers, so numerous bodies were buried in mass graves. This lack of ceremony caused yet further anguish for the survivors who wanted respect paid to their loved ones.

Yet imagine for a moment the situation from the other side, that is, from the perspective of those who had been caught unaware by the tsunami. Most drowned when the huge wave struck. In the normal course of life people generally know that they will die. Whether from disease, old age, or the effect of a fatal wound, the majority of the dying have an opportunity to ready themselves for death. But what happens when people do not have that opportunity?

If one maintains that individual human consciousness is wholly and only a function of the body's brain, the answer is straight forward: nothing happens. An individual body dies, the light of their awareness goes out, and that's the end of that person. Forever. But what if the body dies but the light of individual awareness does not "go out"? What if it continues?

In his account of his out-of-body experiences, William Buhlman described how he appeared to possess an energetic body that was similar to his physical body in size and shape. Furthermore, the energetic world that body occupied was very similar to the physical world. And while he was in his energetic body he could view his physical body.

Let's imagine for a moment that this same experience occurs to people whose bodies, without warning, suddenly die. Having had no opportunity to appreciate that they would soon die, having not eased themselves into an acceptance of what was about to happen, how would they feel? Abruptly disembodied yet still possessing a human awareness, they would likely feel the same as the survivors: traumatised. Like the living, they would feel loss, fear as to what would happen next, perhaps anger at their changed circumstances, even shame or guilt that their loved ones needed help but they were unable to do anything. If they were now experiencing what Buhlman experienced in his first OOB, they would also be feeling very confused about where they were and what this state was that they now found themselves in. It appears that these feelings did in fact occur among the newly deceased.

Reverend Taio Kaneda is a Buddhist priest whose temple is forty-eight kilometres from the coast. Over the days, then the weeks, after the tsunami struck, he made himself available to people to come and talk to him and his fellow monks about how they felt. He called these meetings Café de Monku—in Japanese *monku* means complaint, and the phrase is also a pun on the English word, monk. These talks gave people an opportunity to express their anxiety and fears, as well as to talk about the reasons for their sleeplessness and depression. Because Japanese culture encourages suppressing emotions, the situation helped many release their grief and tears.

However, numerous people also told stories of hauntings, of feeling other people were present among them. Many saw ghosts. Journalist Richard Lloyd Parry visited the north and spoke to Reverend Kaneda. Parry writes of those who talked to the monks:

> They described sightings of ghostly strangers, friends and neighbours, and dead loved ones. They reported hauntings at home, at work, in offices and public places, on the beaches and in the ruined towns. The experiences ranged from eerie dreams and feelings of vague unease to cases of outright possession. A young man complained of pressure on his chest at night, as if some creature was straddling him as he slept. A teenage girl spoke of a fearful figure who squatted in her house. A middle-aged man hated to go out in the rain, because the eyes of the dead stared out at him from puddles.
>
> A fire station in Tagajo received calls to places where all the houses had been destroyed by the tsunami. The crews went out to the ruins anyway and prayed for the spirits of those who had died—and the ghostly calls ceased.
>
> At a refugee community in Onagawa, an old neighbour would appear in the living rooms of the temporary houses,

and sit down for a cup of tea with their startled occupants. No one had the heart to tell her that she was dead; the cushion on which she had sat was wet with seawater.

It is easy to dismiss such experiences as fantasies, as projections of loss, guilt, fear. The Shinto ancestor cult is still widely practised in Japan, so while few Japanese consider themselves religious, many regularly make offerings on behalf of deceased family members. This sense of the continuity of the dead in the hearts of the living may certainly have given rise to the widespread phenomena of ghostly appearances. Then for Reverend Kaneda something more complex occurred.

One evening a young woman was brought to Kaneda's temple. She was a nurse, and neither she nor any of her family had personally suffered from the tsunami. But for several weeks she had felt presences around her. She even felt something was trying to enter her. Understandably, she had been distressed for days. Kaneda responded the same way he did with all those who sought his help: with open-minded concern.

Rumiko was slumped over the table. She stirred as Kaneda addressed the creature within her. "I asked: 'Who are you, and what do you want?'" he said. "When it spoke, it didn't sound like her at all. It talked for three hours."

It was the spirit of a young woman whose mother had divorced and remarried, and who found herself unloved and unwanted by her new family. She ran away and found work in the mizu shobai, or "water trade", the night-time world of clubs, bars, and prostitution. There she became more and more isolated and depressed, and fell under the influence of a morbid and manipulative man. Unknown to her family, unmourned by anyone, she killed herself. Since then, not a stick of incense had been lit in her memory.

Kaneda asked the spirit: "Will you come with me? Do you want me to lead you to the light?" He took her to the main hall of the temple, where he recited the sutra and sprinkled holy water. By the time the prayers were done, at half past one in the morning, Rumiko had returned to herself, and she and her family went home.

Three days later Rumiko returned with the feeling yet another spirit was nearby and attempting to enter her. Kaneda suggested she let it in. She did and Kaneda found himself talking to a sailor who had died during the Second World War. Over the next several weeks, another twenty-five spirits, all killed by the tsunami, spoke through the young woman. One man had committed suicide when he learned his daughters had both died. Another was worried that his wife, who had survived, would kill herself. At first, Rumiko was at the mercy of the spirits. But gradually she learned to control their access. Eventually the visitations ceased and she and her fiance left the area.

The intense situation had an emotional toll on both Rumiko and the priest. Yet as a result of the repeated possessions both developed an ability to help the deceased. Just as the Café de Monku gave a voice to the living and helped relieve their distress, during the spirit sessions the Rumiko became a conduit for lost and confused human spirits, enabling them to share their doubts and fears and to emotionally clear themselves. The Buddhist ceremony Kaneda performed afterwards freed the spirits to move on.

Such an account may be dismissed as involving the imaginations of all involved. Yet situations in which the living help the deceased become reconciled to their new situation is far from uncommon. Another example provides an alternative perspective on this same phenomena of the living helping the deceased.

TALKING TO THE DECEASED

A meditation group in Hamilton, New Zealand, has for several years been facilitating what they term "soul rescues". The group is directed by Peter Calvert, a meditator and channeller. The procedure is that group members sit in meditation for a time, making themselves available for contact. One by one, although sometimes simultaneously, spirits then appear. Some find their own way to the group, evidently attracted by the energy being sent out. Others are guided there by other spirits.

For several years, the group has recorded and transcribed what occurs between the spirits and the meditators. The following exchange is typical of the process. This particular soul rescue began with one of the meditators sensing that a spirit was screaming at her. An exchange between the screaming spirit and the meditators then began. The italicised voice is the spirit speaking through one of the meditators. The other voices are those of the meditators. The meditator who had initially heard the scream began by telling the spirit to look around and realise she is dead. She also told the spirit that she didn't need to scream any more, that her torment was over. The spirit responded:

Ok, now what do I do? If I'm not in pain any more, what do I do?

Do you understand that you are dead, you don't have a body any more?

Somebody just told me that.

Are you ready to go on to the next stage?

If there is a next stage.

There is indeed. First tell us what happened to you.

I was burnt and hung. There's something around my neck. I was fighting. There was a fire, I could smell tar, something on my skin.

What country were you in?

Jamaica. I'm black.

What year?

1857.

You've been in limbo a long time. The next stage is for someone to come and get you.

I don't want anyone to come and get me! Oh, no! They've already got me!

They can't harm you any more.

I don't want to go anywhere. I've had enough pain. I don't want any more.

The person who comes to get you might be one of your loved ones. Is there anyone you'd like to see again?

I don't know anything about love. Nobody ever cared a thing about me.

Was there somebody that you respected?

Only my dog. The only one that ever cared about me.

Did you have brothers and sister?

No.

Your parents weren't there for you?

No. I don't remember anything about my childhood, only my dog.

Well, perhaps call for your dog. Call his name, and look upwards, towards the light.

What if I can hear him barking?

That's promising. Can you see the light?

No.

Look upwards and see if you can see the light, and see your dog.

What about all the chains they put around me?

If you don't have a body, they don't matter, do they?

They said I was evil, and that I would go to hell, so I had chains and shackles and fire.

Do you have them now?

No.

So you can move yourself. You can go anywhere you want.

I think you're talking nonsense. I was told I was evil.

Did you believe them?

They told me. I must have been. They tarred me and lit me and burned me alive, so I must have been.

Did you feel that you were bad?

I never did nothing wrong.

Well, there you are. You're not evil, are you?

Well, who's to judge? They're the ones that did it to me.

That was back then, this is now. This is different. You have no chains. You're free to go wherever you choose, or to stay.

I guess there's nothing to stay for.

Would you like your dog as a companion?

Yes, if I could find him again.

Call him the way you used to call him, and look for him.

There are some steps leading out of here, to a doorway. They might just catch me on the other side and do it again.

They can't harm you. You no longer have a body, so you can't be harmed. So just go up the steps.

Ok. I guess if my dog's there it'll be ok. Hey, there's some other folks there, same skin as me. They're waving at me to come.

Is your dog there too?

Yep. They're not burning me, it must be ok.

Yes. (Gone.)

According to information received by the group, when their body dies most people's awareness slips easily into the afterlife state. But some people become confused, due to social or religious programming, personal fear, or because they don't appreciate that their body has died. This suggests we carry dominant ideas and attitudes with us into the afterlife. If those ideas are negative or limiting in some way, and if we haven't worked through and resolved them sufficiently during our life, then we may be dominated by them during the initial period after the body's death. Those concepts dominate until we realise our mistake.

Other spirits who have come to this group include a coal miner who had been trapped underground by a fall and had been sitting in the dark for over a century. Another was a small boy who was murdered and had been hiding ever since, scared his killers would return. So accident and malicious intent also impact psychologically on the deceased. However, often the situation is quite innocuous.

What are all you people doing here? What are you all sitting around for?

To be of service to people who come along. How can we help you?

How you can possibly help me? Really! I don't know. What are you doing here? I just saw you all sitting around. I don't know how I got here, I just did.

Have you been on your own for some time?

I think I have. I don't know how long, but I think I have.

Where were you before?

Well, I was very happy. I was busy. I looked after people. I spent my whole life running around looking after people. I was useful and not a busybody as such, but I was busy in a helpful way. And all of a sudden I'm not busy, I'm just sitting around, and it's terribly boring. I don't know what happened. I was busy, and then I stopped.

We might be able to solve that problem for you, because it seems that you no longer have a body, and you've died.

Oh, goodness. I remember lying in a hospital bed. I don't remember lying there, but I remember looking down and seeing myself lying there, with everyone around me crying. Oh, my goodness.

I guess that was your spirit rising up out of your body.

Well, that was a long time ago!

What year?

1963!

It's probably time you moved on to the next step. Do you know what that is?

No. I don't know what to do.

Some people from your past, people who have died and gone before you, will come and take you to the next stage. Who would you like to meet up with?

This is strange. I can see some people waving in the distance that I hadn't seen before!

That's probably the ones that are looking for you.

I was looking down, but they're up over there!

Just take yourself over and greet them. Be on your way with our blessings.

That would be alright? I'm worried about my body. But I don't need to worry about that any more?

No, you don't have a body, just leave it behind. It's a bit sad really, isn't it? But it's served its purpose. You don't need it any more. You can go and join the others.

I do feel quite light, I suppose.

Move your spirit and consciousness over to those people who are waiting. You can go quickly.
You're sure it's alright?
Yes, go and see them.
Okay. (Gone.)

ACKNOWLEDGING THE EXTRA-LIVING

I began this chapter by observing that if our awareness extends beyond our biologically and socially constructed identity, what and who do we interact with? Michael Harner's shamanic experiences, the accounts of interactions with the surprised and disconcerted dead after the Japanese tsunami, and the New Zealand meditation group's records of soul rescues, provide three answers to this question. They suggest an alignment exists between embodied human awareness and non-embodied spirits that is much more real and direct than is commonly assumed in Western culture.

Most of us are raised to think there is a barrier between the living and the so-called dead—which, given the above accounts, do not appear to be dead at all, and so can perhaps more accurately now be referred to as the extra-living. What these examples suggest is that the barrier between us and the extra-living is a socially generated construct. Moreover, it takes a punctured reality experience for us to realise that the barrier *is* constructed

Of course, once the barrier comes down interactions between the living and the extra-living may become fraught, as occurred in Japan after the tsunami, due to confusion on both sides of the communications. Perhaps even more problematic are conversations between those who have demolished the barrier and those who consider the barrier doesn't exist—on the grounds that there is no "other side" and certainly no "extra-living" who occupy that realm.

This gap in appreciation is crucial to all discussions regarding the nature of extended reality and of the extra-living. Those raised in traditional cultures, who have been exposed to a shamanistic perspective, see no barrier. They perceive the material and immaterial, the physical and spiritual, individual body and personal spirit, as equally contributing to human existence. The human and what is colloquially known as "the spooky" are accepted as two aspects of a continuous reality. In contrast, in the West, and in many religiously structured cultures, the spooky is problematic, because people have been socially conditioned to view the extra-living as ghosts—and ghosts are terrifying. For those living in such cultures, the spooky has been demonised. On the other hand, for convinced materialists the situation is problematic in another way, because for them the spooky doesn't exist at all.

CHAPTER TWELVE

Spooky Stuff at a Distance

GHOSTS ENTERING PEOPLE and complaining about what has happened to them, a man putting his hand through the bedroom wall, another seeing far away places in his mind, others accurately dreaming of events before they happen, yet others travelling outside their body—these events are not part of our ordinary notions of what is possible. They are not part of what we ordinarily think of as what happens in reality. Yet people report being active participants in these and many other kinds of non-ordinary experiences. The minimal conclusion is that human reality is not as it appears to be.

If we accept that non-ordinary experiences are possible, if we take such experiences seriously, then they require us to re-evaluate how we think reality and consciousness are constituted. Clearly, not everyone *is* willing to take such experiences seriously. Even fewer wish to engage in a total review of their world view, given it may end up overturning what they have long accepted as real. Nonetheless, this is what the discoveries of the new mysticism ask of us. They challenge us to redefine our view of reality and rethink what human consciousness is capable of doing.

SPOOKING AGREED REALITY

Seriously allowing that non-ordinary experiences are possible requires us to loosen our grip on agreed reality. The task of redefining the scope of mysticism starts with being willing *psychologically* to expand our meta-explanations of what constitutes reality and our assumptions regarding what human awareness is able to perceive and do. In the face of the reports offered in the previous chapters, and given the innumerable similar reports available in historical and contemporary records, we need to allow that, to adapt Einstein's famous saying, spooky stuff occurs at a considerable distance from where we base ourselves—which is safely within the confines of locally agreed reality.

The problem, again psychologically, is that people are so attached to their notions of agreed reality that, faced with experiences that are not just non-ordinary but are outlandish, and that are potentially devastating personally to their notion of identity and professionally to their career, they aren't able to cope with the implications of the new information. They enter a state of cognitive dissonance, and as they strive to return to their previous equilibrium they view the new data as spooky and reject it. Fear is commonly behind this rejection, given fear leads people to equate spooky stuff with scary stuff. Clearly, fear is a natural human response. Psychologically, letting go of what we know is scary. As both William Buhlman and Joseph McMoneagle observed, overcoming fear is a crucial first step to successfully exploring the non-ordinary aspects of reality.

So fear and denial are a psychological given. But what is the alternative? What about when the spooky isn't viewed as scary but is instead embraced as a valid part of reality? Traditional cultures, especially those that still acknowledge shamanic beliefs and practices, are structured according to an agreed reality that willingly includes seeing deceased ancestors, travelling outside one's body, and interacting with spirits. Shamanic meta-explanations of the world consider that reality consists of both body and spirit. In the shamanic world view spirits are everywhere. All places and all creatures are seen as being animated by spiritual identities. The result is that in traditional shamanic cultures spooky stuff isn't scary, it's just how reality is, and it isn't distant because it's present in parallel to the activities of everyday life.

As I have argued throughout, two factors have led to a cultural repudiation of the traditional spooky-embracing shamanic world view. The first is Christianity, which has long demonised anything that happens outside the fences erected by Church ritual and doctrine. As a result, in the West the traditional shaman was reduced to the magician and the witch, who were then denigrated on the grounds they were playing on the Devil's team. The second denying factor is scientific naturalism, which maintains that anything spooky is an illusion.

Consolidating Western concepts of agreed reality is that where traditional shamanic cultures happily clapped with two hands, that is, freely joined body and spirit, Christianity maintains that its defining spiritual activity occurred in the distant past, during the period Christ and his apostles lived, and will recur in the future, when the world ends. In maintaining this view they tie one hand of their awareness behind their backs, excluding it from their current life. Meanwhile, scientific naturalists maintain there is only one hand, that of the natural world. Ironically, it is the clapping produced when one-handed Western religion meets one-handed Western science that has created the polarised view of reality in which we are all brought up today.

WHEN THE SPOOKY IS REJECTED

As I noted earlier, the notion of polarised reality—that consciousness and matter, subjective mind and objectively existing body, are completely separate realms of reality—was first proposed by René Descartes. Descartes initiated a decisive intellectual break from pre-modern religious and mythological explanations of the world when he separated the thinking soul from its physical body and argued that scientific laws are sufficient to reveal what underpins physical reality.

While later scientific thinkers agreed with Descartes that only the sciences can uncover the nature of physical reality, the majority also came to reject Descartes' notion of a thinking soul existing in a spiritual realm. Biologists directed the light of enquiry into the body, searched for Descartes' ghost, and found nothing inside—no mind, no awareness, no individual intent of any kind. I noted earlier that Gilbert Ryles spoke on behalf of the twentieth century intellectual consensus when he called Descartes' ghostly soul in the machinery of the body a colossal error. Philosopher David Lewis hammered this view home when he asserted: "We grant there are possible spooky worlds where materialism is false, but we insist that our actual world isn't one of them."

From the materialist perspective all we have inside us is a brain made of pulsing meat through which chemicals surge and electricity sparks. How, then, does our sense of being a subjectively experiencing identity arise? Biologist E.O. Wilson has answered this question by proposing that our perceptions are processed by neural networks. These networks generate a range of possible responsive scenarios, then select one or more scenario to act on. All this occurs automatically—because no one is actually at home to do the thinking:

> The mind is a self-organising republic of scenarios that individually germinate, grow, evolve, disappear, and occasionally linger to spawn additional thought and physical activity. ... Who or what within the brain monitors all this activity? No one. Nothing. The scenarios are not seen by some other part of the brain. They just *are*. Consciousness is the virtual world composed by scenarios. There is not even a Cartesian theatre, to use Daniel Dennett's dismissive phrase, no single locus of the brain where the scenarios are played out in coherent form. Instead there are interlacing patterns of neural activity. ... In ways still not understood, [each] pattern is coupled with simultaneous input from other parts of the brain to create the full scenarios of consciousness. The biologist S.J. Singer has drily expressed the matter thus: I link, therefore I am.

So Descartes' ghost has been replaced by neural scenarios spontaneously arising in a meat brain animated by chemicals and electricity. We may feel we are an identity that is born, lives a life, makes choices, develops relationships, variously cares or doesn't care about what happens around it and to the people it meets. Yet, according to Wilson and his fellow naturalists, the subjective feeling we have of actually existing is a delusion. All that actually exists is a haze of neural static. In the middle of the neural buzz no one is home. None of us are here.

SCIENTISM VS THE SCIENTIFIC METHOD

The endpoint of the materialist approach is to reduce all collective and personal human achievement to neural static, and to acknowledge only what is a substance and can be explained using the tenets of scientific naturalism. Individual consciousness is crossed off the list of actually existing things because it isn't a substance you can pin, slice and dice.

The examples given in the previous chapters show the limitation of adopting a purely naturalistic approach. They provide counter-data that suggest identity cannot be reduced to neural twitches. Besides Eben Alexander's near death experience, the ghosts who appeared after Japan's tsunami, and the confused disembodied people who talked to the Hamilton meditators, there are many other instances on record that affirm awareness and identity are not limited to bodily and neural processes and that they do not expire when the body dies.

The increasing numbers of contemporary records suggest that awareness and identity are more complex phenomena than hardcore materialists allow. The naturalist project of reducing mindful awareness to the brain, identity to behaviour, and an individual's life endeavours to neural static, falls well short of explaining the multi-levelled phenomena that being human involves. Any explanation that has no way of accounting for human subjectivity, and that does not encompass the entire range of human experiencing, ordinary and non-ordinary, is inadequate. Dismissing subjective experience on the grounds it is not objective, or is unscientific, or is irrelevant, or is simply fantasy, is too simple-minded. Too much data is on record for the dismissive naturalist attitude to be accepted any longer.

A fundamental issue is that when people consider mystical, paranormal, and occult experiences, critics and doubters adopt a *scientistic* and not a *scientific* approach. Scientism involves maintaining that reality is wholly and only constituted of matter, and that only the sciences are adequate to understand the material world. The scientistic approach denigrates all the other approaches human beings adopt when exploring and striving to understand reality. This is the disaster of modernity that Ken Wilber drew attention to, the substituting of the premodern dogmatic, religious outlook with an equally dogmatic materialist modern or post-modern outlook.

Scientism presents a problem because it has been smuggled into Western culture and today underpins it intellectually in exactly the same way that Christianity underpinned European culture until Enlightenment thinkers challenged its premises. Today's intellectuals, cultural writers, critics, educators, and leaders of all kinds, who promote dealing with the "real world" and who in so doing automatically denigrate anything spooky, are proselytising a dogmatic description of the world. Because what exactly is the "real world"? It is not the same as the "agreed world". Until this issue is addressed, all theories, stances, descriptions, and prohibitions around what is valid data and what is invalid data remain moot.

This brings us back to the psychological issue of people having a vested interest in their particular variety of agreed reality and not being willing to countenance alternative perspectives. Until the positions of deniers such as Ray Hyman are themselves critiqued, and it is appreciated how much denial is driven by psychological and social rather than by scientific factors, little progress will be made in publicly acknowledging the advances that investigators into non-ordinary phenomena have made. That their advances remain unacknowledged reflects the extent to which the scientistic attitude holds scientists, educators, and public intellectuals in thrall.

In contrast, the *scientific method* is agnostic. It remains open and makes no automatic meta-assumptions in relation to observational data. Those practising the scientific method deal with the data at hand and draw rational conclusions without needing to reject data that contradicts previously agreed positions. Just as Descartes and his fellow Enlightenment thinkers strategised and fought in order to free themselves from the constraints placed on them by the orthodox of their day, so today's advance explorers of human subjective experiences are struggling to free themselves from the constraints placed on them by the scientistic orthodox who demand that all statements made about reality conform with the tenets of naturalism. Clearly, the Enlightenment drive to obtain knowledge not tainted by assumptions inherited from the past has not yet achieved its goal. Much still remains to be dismantled so we may continue to freely explore and clarify.

One major area of research is to reconsider all received notions of what constitutes the spiritual domain. Instead of demonising certain subjective experiences, or denying they occur, we need to re-evaluate the data that is being unearthed regarding spiritual and psychological phenomena, including contentious phenomena such as people talking to spirits or using spirits for personal guidance or to heal. This leads to the issue of mediumship, a major aspect of spirit-human interactions, which has historically underpinned shamanic activities, that has not yet been discussed here.

THE MEDIUM DELIVERS THE MESSAGE

Mediumship has a reputation for being a theatrical show put on by charlatans who cynically exploit gullible people's desire to believe. This attitude dates back to the Victorian era, when researchers first began to seriously investigate anomalous psychological phenomena without prejudging the results—and when debunkers vociferously did just that.

In fact, mediumship has a long history. The ancient Greek Pythia who for two thousand years provided the voice for the oracle at Delphi is a widely famed example. Today mediumship manifests in diverse forms: spirit possession in Haitian vodou, stage mediums who facilitate communication between the living and dead, the many channelled identities who have followed in the footsteps of Jane Roberts' Seth, and television mediums who help police solve murders.

Technically, a medium is a material or substance that facilitates the exchange of information from one state or situation to another. A language is a medium by which one person talks to another. A book is a medium by which thoughts, feelings, and experiences are communicated. Priests are mediums because they act as a conduit between the spiritual and human realms. A classical musician is a medium who translates composed music for an audience.

In the same way, whenever a human being seeks to communicate with spirits, a medium is required. That medium is human awareness. This may sound scary: Someone has to open their awareness to a spirit? Isn't that dangerous? Yet we open our awareness to others every moment of every day. And we equally close down our awareness when we don't like what is coming at us. That is choice in operation. Choice equally applies to communicating with spirits. Those who choose to talk to spirits open themselves up, even if they don't do the communicating themselves and instead use another person to communicate with spirits on their behalf—a person who functions as a medium.

All this means that mediumship is far more common than we generally acknowledge. In the context of spiritual communications, mediumship doesn't only apply to conversing with the extra-living. Many families have an aunt, or a grandfather, or a cousin, who has second sight, or is psychic, or just knows things they should not logically be able to. They are mediums who channel non-everyday knowledge. The aunt who "knows things" wouldn't be called a shaman by their family or those who have her to do a reading for them, yet her intuitions fall within the scope of what a traditional shaman does. Accordingly, it could be said that the fundamental difference between traditional tribal cultures and modern cultures is not that there are more spiritual mediums in the first and fewer in the second. The difference is that tribal cultures acknowledge human exchanges with spirits where modern cultures do not.

Traditional and modern mediums say mediumship occurs for one straightforward reason: the spirit realm does not exist at a distance from the human. In contradistinction to Descartes' dualistic concept of soul and body existing in separate realms, their view is that the spirit realm exists beside the physical. Contact between the two realms is possible because at their core every human being is a subjectively experiencing immaterial consciousness.

Accordingly, whoever opens themselves up to communication is able to access the spirit realm. In fact, whether we realise it or not, many of us *have* accessed that realm. This occurs whenever we have a punctured reality experience in which some aspect of non-ordinary reality has manifested into the fabric of our everyday existence. However distractions, social programming, fear, or wanting to conform to agreed norms, ensures we mostly ignore, forget, or suppress our memories of non-ordinary occurrences. Distraction is arguably the most prevalent factor given that, in the rush of life, memories of subtle and suggestive occurrences are simply swept away and their implications are not followed up.

Underpinning all this is that human awareness is itself a medium via which communications regularly extend from spirit to body and back again. The exchanges between the Hamilton meditators and confused spirits suggest that after a person dies their awareness continues intact into the afterlife state, with people sustaining their prior emotions, thoughts, and attitudes, including their mental assumptions and adopted constructs regarding the nature or non-existence of the extra-living realm itself.

Accordingly, on the one hand, awareness can function as a medium by which spirits communicate to human beings. In this sense, each individual's awareness is a medium via which information is passed from the spirit realm to the physical human realm. Equally, awareness also functions as a medium via which experiences and information gleaned while living in the human world may be transferred to the spirit realm. Hence human awareness is a medium that involves a two-way transfer.

All this suggests it is possible to propose a new definition of mysticism. It could be said that mystics are those who are aware that information is passing through their awareness in both directions, from spirit to body and from body to spirit. And mystics have pragmatically developed procedures, which work personally for them, for accessing and facilitating that two-way information exchange.

The Music of Two Hands

CHAPTER THIRTEEN

Requirements for Future Progress

THE INDIAN POET Kabir joked that human beings ignore the spiritual dimension in the same way that fish ignore the sea. His point is that what is most fundamental to our existence—our radically subjective awareness—is also the most hidden, not because it is inaccessible but because it is so inescapably present that we ignore it. Caught up in the minute-by-minute sensations of daily life, we ignore the greater reality in which our awareness bobs, dives, and swims.

Deep sea diving, penetrating deep into the interiors of our existence, is never easily done. Focused informed effort is required. This is the work mystics have been doing for millennia, beginning with ancient shamans. As cultures became more complex, sophisticated religious beliefs and social structures were laid over shamanistic procedures, requiring mystics to re-frame their explorations within—and sometimes in opposition to—religious and social norms.

In the Victorian era phenomenological and empirical approaches were developed to investigate non-ordinary aspects of the human psyche. The authors of the British Society for Psychical Research's *Phantasms of the Living* were optimistic that the data they published would initiate serious discussions of paranormal phenomena. If they were alive today they would be hugely disappointed. The advances they hoped for have not eventuated.

While progress since their pioneering study has been significant in a number of areas, professional and public acknowledgement of that progress has been minimal. Scepticism and denial, the default positions adopted in scientific and intellectual circles during the twentieth century, continue to dominate this century's public attitudes towards non-ordinary phenomena.

Rather than extending the work of the nineteenth century Society for Psychical Research and seeking to explore the depths of human awareness, during the twentieth century Western intellectual culture went in the opposite direction, developing a skin-deep materialist interpretation of reality that deliberately denied the depth components of human experience. Ken Wilber calls this outlook flatland, the disastrously limited philosophy of modernity. It views life as surface-skating functionalism, with consciousness an illusory by-product of brain activity and identity is considered to involve only biological, chemical and social factors. Individual awareness is snuffed out when the body of which it is an epiphenomenon dies.

This twentieth century naturalistic prescription has not been confirmed by empirical research. While many scientists agree with E.O. Wilson that it is only a matter of time before their naturalistic view is confirmed, today it remains a meta-explanation that uses guesswork to stitch together biological, chemical and psychological phenomena.

THREE PROBLEMS FOR NATURALISM

The twentieth century naturalist perspective is guesswork because all the available data about human existence has not yet been gathered. Fields of research are not static. Each decade brings new data and insights. Theories are proposed to account for the available data, refined to accommodate further data, then put aside when they no longer explain all the data.

As a result, no scientific theory is a final theory. All scientific theories are working theories. Because much data has not been collected, they offer incompletely informed propositions regarding what may be the case. This is seen in E.O. Wilson's explanation of how consciousness is generated. He asserts his theory is likely to be valid, while admitting scientists currently lack sufficient evidence to support his explanation for how a brain made of meat, chemicals and electricity actually generates self-awareness and subjectivity.

A second problem for naturalism is that when scientists attempt to explain immaterial phenomena such as self-awareness and subjectivity few agree with one another, offering quite different models to account for how they arise. This lack of agreement indicates how much scientists are formulating meta-scientific speculations that are guesses based on shared naturalistic assumptions about reality.

The third difficulty is that naturalists reject data that does not fit with their assumptions. Mystical phenomena are ignored or explained away as occurring naturally. Some hardcore critics flatly deny mystical phenomena occur at all, going so far as to impugn the professionalism of those investigating such phenomena..

Given these three factors—the scope of what we do not know; that there are no universally agreed theories that account for consciousness, subjectivity and non-ordinary perceptions; and that the immaterial is excluded from scientific accounts of human experience—current materialist pronouncements about our human situation can only be guesswork, however educated that guesswork may be.

In the meantime, refusing to admit outlier data is a disingenuous way to proceed. It is scientistic rather than scientific.

EMBRACING THE ANOMALOUS

In the sciences, data that is inconsistent with agreed reality, and so reveals deficiencies in current models and theories, is willingly embraced. During the search for the Higgs boson particle scientists hoped they would record unexpected phenomena not accounted for by the standard model of sub-atomic particles. On the one hand, scientists require results that confirm their models, because that tells them they are on the right track. On the other, they value anomalies because data that stretches or contradicts their models reveals new areas for research, which in turn leads to new knowledge. Without anomalies research would become static and no new discoveries would be made.

Surveys undertaken by Robert Forman, David Hay and the UK-based The Religious Experience Research Centre suggest that around half of the Western population has had an anomalous paranormal or mystical experience. Their surveys also reveal that most keep quiet about such experiences because they are publicly taboo topics and they don't want their social or professional status to be tainted by accusations that they have "jumped the fence".

But what if all of us have *already* jumped the fence? What if the radical subjectivity at the core of our human experience *already* situates a part of our awareness beyond the boundaries erected by socially agreed reality? What if we are *already* swimming in the depths?

All existence consists of a vastness of which we consciously experience only a tiny portion. Those who have jumped over the fences that demarcate agreed reality from what lies beyond, who have opened a crack in the world and stepped through—whether they are a modern shaman who meets spirits in a cave, a young nurse who finds herself invaded by the angry deceased, or a doctor who is inexplicably visited by precognitive dreams—are all standing at the edge of an ocean of perceptual possibilities.

Just as scientists assume no theoretical limits to the ways they can explore, manipulate, and transform the physical world, so it is appropriate that today's mystics assume no theoretical limits to the ways they may explore, manipulate, and transform their own subjective awareness. The only limits in either case are the limits generated by the human mind. And these limits are progressively, if somewhat slowly, falling away.

THE NEW MYSTICAL APPROACH

The psychological and phenomenological approaches adopted by practitioners of the new mysticism present an opportunity to escape intellectual straightjackets, whether naturalistic or religious, and process anomalous experiences using whatever parameters practitioners find useful. The following seven characteristics identify the ways new mystical practitioners are proceeding.

o   *A phenomenological approach.* The new mysticism is grounded in personal experience. It focuses on what is encountered during heightened states of awareness.

o *A developmental process.* Practices are designed to help aspirants transform their awareness in order to enter heightened states.

o *Bottom-up conceptualising.* All explanations and conceptualising are derived from the data of experience.

o *Grassroots engagement.* The social structure that facilitates all this is grassroots. Where institutional approaches to spirituality require aspirants to fit their experiences into top-down conceptual frameworks, a grassroots approach is bottom-up and accordingly adjusts easily and quickly to accommodate new experiences. As a result, the grassroots approach is personal, open, fluid and non-dogmatic.

o *Experimental in practice.* A phenomenological approach and openness in thinking generates an experimental approach to explorations. Practices are tried and continued or dropped on the basis of effectiveness. The aspirant's own awareness is the laboratory where experiments take place.

o *Testing is ongoing.* All results are tested. Testing may involve one person repeating the same experiment, or numbers of people each carrying out the same experiment and comparing results.

o *Results are provisional.* Whatever results are achieved are viewed not as providing final truths but as offering provisional truths. These provisional truths will do until a fuller explanation is arrived at. There is always a fuller explanation.

ADVANCING THE NEW MYSTICISM

We live at the start of the twenty-first century, in a historical period when long-accepted world views have crumbled and many people are seeking new explanations for how reality is constituted and how the multiple layers of human consciousness interact to generate awareness and identity.

A new perspective is needed, an alternative to the outmoded, partial, or orthodox, whether the orthodox be religious, Neo-Darwinist, modernist, post-modernist, or naturalist. In shaping this new perspective we need to resist the temptation to adopt broad sweeping explanations of the human situation using overly simplistic premises, whether they be material, immaterial, psychological, or spiritual. We also need to avoid intellectual and professional posturing, along with ploys to protect territory, status and reputations. The ways that psychological traits limit progress, particularly within professional environments, is rarely acknowledged. Those dominated by self-defensive psychological traits are currently erecting major barriers to progress. The challenge is to keep the discussion open and fluid and for it not to be closed down by those who rule that certain issues have already been explained or dictate that particular areas of research are out-of-bounds. Three conditions need to be fulfilled for progress to be made.

First, we can only seriously start investigating heightened states of awareness, and analysing the various phenomena human beings experience in such states, when broad-based agreement has been reached regarding what actually constitutes a mystical experience. To achieve this, categories encompassing every possible variety of heightened experience need to be established, incorporating the mystically self-transcendent, the parapsychological, the occult, and all other related subjective phenomena and experiences.

Second, agreed protocols for identifying, labelling, categorising, and analysing subjective experiences are required. This is urgent because while protocols for collecting and collating hard physical data have been developed over the last three hundred years, protocols for collecting and collating subjective data have only been developed in recent decades. While useful progress in collecting qualitative data has been made in the fields of the social sciences and anthropology, personal testimonies of non-ordinary states continue to be dismissed on the grounds they are anecdotal. When one person claims their awareness left their body during a near death experience we may doubt their testimony, but when thousands of people attest to the same experience dismissal on anecdotal grounds is no longer a valid response. Investigation is required. To create a balanced research environment, qualitative data needs to be accorded equal status to quantitative data.

Third, in order for such studies to progress, the resistance generated by those who adhere to the dominant scientistic outlook needs to be overcome, along with the hostility of those who have personal and professional motives for denying the existence and significance of non-ordinary perceptions.

These three issues are interlinked. One cannot be resolved without the other two being simultaneously addressed. Naturally, it will take considerable effort by significant numbers of people over an extended period—likely decades—for the radical aspects of non-ordinary subjective experiencing to be appreciated as a valid field for research and for progress to be made in establishing satisfactory investigative protocols.

Meanwhile, mystics working outside the mainstream are making their own discoveries as they quietly explore outlier experiences.

THE MUSIC OF TWO HANDS

The spooky is present more than we publicly acknowledge. Those involved in the new mysticism are developing tools appropriate to the twenty-first century to explore the implications of this realisation. However, uncritical acceptance of the spooky, and easy explanations of what is involved, are as unsatisfactory as prejudiced, fear-fuelled rejections and intellectually lazy dismissals. We require a new perspective that supports those who are explor subjective states. We also urgently need to develop an investigative process that balances openness with scepticism, and especially to begin evaluating subjectively obtained data honestly and insightfully, without pre-judgement.

Only when we are able to acknowledge subjectivity equally with objectivity, and only when the spooky is normalised as just another way to experience reality, will we be able to accept that our existence encompasses two hands clapping, and that the music those two hands make is fundamental to what each of us experiences throughout our life. It is a music that has the potential to be informative as well as moving—provided we first are willing to open our ears to its sound.

References

CHAPTER ONE: CLAPPING WITH TWO HANDS?

— The "miraculous" is very difficult to define

P.D. Ouspensky, *In Search of the Miraculous*, NY: Harcourt (1949), p 3.

CHAPTER TWO: THE PROBLEM WITH MYSTICISM

— We don't want to mix science and religion

John Geirland, *Buddha on the Brain: The Hot New Topic of Neuroscience: Meditation!*, Wired, Issue 14.02 (2006).

— We are machines built by DNA

Richard Dawkins, *The Ultraviolet Garden*, Royal Institute Christmas Lecture, No. 4, (1991).

— This is Descartes' error: the abyssal separation

Antonia R. Damasio, *Descartes' Error: Emotion, Reason and the Human Brain*, N.Y.: Avon Books (1994), pp 249-250.

— I hope to prove that it is entirely false

Gilbert Ryle, *The Concept of Mind*, London: Hutchinson (1949), p 16.

— I have a physician friend who frequently speaks

Larry Dossey M.D., *Reinventing Medicine: Byond Body-Mind to a New Era of Healing*, San Francisco: HarperSanFransisco (2000), p 11.

CHAPTER FIVE: THE SYMBOLIC LANGUAGE OF ALCHEMY

— He was the last of the magicians

John Maynard Keynes, *Newton, the Man*, in *Essays in Biography* (2nd ed., 1951), pp 311-4.

— When once my mind was meditating

G.R.S. Meade, *Thrice Greatest Hermes: Studies in Hellenistic Theosophy and Gnosis*, London: Theosophical Publishing Society (1906). *Poemandres, the Shepherd of Men*, 1.1-4.

— That which is below is like that which is above

Emerald Tablet, Isaac Newton, "Keynes MS. 28". *The Chymistry of Isaac Newton*, edited by William R. Newman (June 2010), <http://webapp1.dlib.indiana.edu/newton/mss/dipl/ALCH00017>.

— The man of copper ... you will not find as a man of copper
Garth Fowden, *The Egyptian Hermes: A Historical Approach to the Pagan Mind*, New Jersey: Princton University Press (1986), p 121.
— Alchemies are here prohibited
Pope John XXII, *De Crimine Falsi Titulus VI. I Joannis XXII*, http://www.levity.com/alchemy/papaldcr.html

CHAPTER SIX: SELF-TRANSFORMATIVE ASCETICISM

— There are just two states for that person
The Upanishads: A New Translation, Vol 3, Swami Nikhilandanda, NY: Ramakrishna-Vivekananda Center (1991). *Brihadaranyaka Upanishad* 4.3.9.
— Casting away the coarseness of the body
Garth Fowden, ibid, p 121.
— The disciplined yogi, living in seclusion
Keith Hill, *Bhagavad Gita*, Attar Books (2006), Discourse 6:10 ff , p 45.
— When the loving kindness of God first calls a soul
Quoted in Evelyn Underhill, *Mysticism*, NY: E.P. Dutton (1913/1961), p 441.
— The first thing in all the arts and sciences
John Cassian, *Conferences*, 1:4. Translated by C.S. Gibson. *From Nicene and Post-Nicene Fathers*, Second Series, Vol. 11. Edited by Philip Schaff and Henry Wace. (Buffalo, NY: Christian Literature Publishing Co., 1894.) Revised and edited for New Advent by Kevin Knight. <http://www.newadvent.org/fathers/350801.htm>.
— I shall make bold to say, my dear brothers
Peter Damian, quoted from Letter 161 in *The Fathers of the Church: Mediaeval Continuation: The Letters of Peter Damien, 151-180*, translated by O. J. Blum OFM and I. M. Resnick, The Catholic Church of America Press (2005), p 133.
— The flagellants saw themselves as redeemers
Barbara W. Tuchman, *A Distant Mirror*, London: Macmillan (1987), p 114.

CHAPTER SEVEN: THE METAPHYSICS OF THE OCCULT

— He is never seen, but is the seer
Swami Nikhilandanda, ibid. *Brihadranyaka Upanishad* 3.7.24
— The rite is a form of yoga
Joseph Campbell, *The Masks of God: Oriental Mythology*, NY: Viking Press Edition (1982), pp 360–361.

— Often I have woken to myself out of the body
Plotinus, *The Neoplatonists*, translated and edited by John Gregory, Kyle Cathy (1991), p 4, Ennead 4.8.
— Whoever are gods in the true sense
Iamblichus, *De Mysteriis*, translated by Emma C. Clarke, John M. Dillon and Jackson P. Hershell, Boston: Brill (2004). Book III.31, pp 197-201.

CHAPTER EIGHT: MAGIC AND ITS DISSENTERS

— The finest emotion of which we are capable
Albert Einstein, *Albert Einstein, the Human Side*, edited by Helen Dukas and Banesh Hoffman, Princeton University Press (1979).

CHAPTER NINE: BURSTING REALITY'S BOUNDARIES

— A handsome Frenchman, such as one might
— My brain plays with a few thoughts
— Conjuring? I dismiss the suggestion as absurd
Paul Brunton, *A Search in Sacred India*, London: Rider (1934), Chapter Three.
— During my first year of medical practice
— I woke in the grey dawn
Larry Dossey M.D., *Reinventing Medicine: Beyond Body-Mind to a New Era of Healing*, San Francisco: HarperSanFransisco (2000), pp 1 ff.
— The moment I understood this
— I was wildly—and naively—eager
Eben Alexander, M.D., *Proof of Heaven: A Neurosurgeon's Journey into the Afterlife*, Sydney: Pan Macmillian (2012), excerpts from pp 29-49 and pp 125-132.

CHAPTER TEN: THE PARANORMAL AS OUTLIER

— As the idea of Telepathy becomes understood
Edmund Gurney, Frederic W. H. Myers, Frank Podmore, *Phantasms of the Living*, London: Rooms of the Society for Pyschical Research (1886), Vol 2, Conclusion 2-3.
— Parapsychology is the scientific and scholarly study
Available on the the Association's website: http://www.parapsych.org
— Many people would rather inflict pain on themselves
AFP, Washington, July 2014.
— The Pain of Doing Nothing: Preferring Negative Stimulation to Boredom, Open Science Network: https://osf.io/nduxr/ (February 16, 2014).

— We don't expect anyone
Erin C. Westgate interviewed by Lindsey Cook, *Shocking: Humans Will Do Anything but Think*, http://www.usnews.com/topics/author/lindsey-cook (July 22, 2014).
— We agree that there is an overall significant effect
— The committee finds no scientific justification
Chris Carter, *Science and Psychic Phenomena: The Fall of the House of Sceptics*, Rochester: Inner Traditions (2nd ed., 2012), pp 96, 18.
— The total human and financial resources
Jessica Utts, *Response to Ray Hyman's Report*, (15 September, 1995), http://www.ics.uci.edu/~jutts/response.html.
— What they got was more than they expected
Joseph McMoneagle, *The Stargate Chronicles*, Crossroad Press (2014), Chapter 8.
— One night about eleven o'clock I drifted off
— Out of curiosity I call out
— As I stare at this man
— An unquenchable desire for knowledge
William Buhlman, *Adventures Beyond the Body*, HarperOne (1996).
— The place where I stood was a corral
Carlos Castaneda, *The Teachings of Don Juan: A Yaqui Way of Knowledge*, Penguin Books (1970), pp 99-100.
— The belief system I was trying to study
— All at once the people in front of me
Carlos Castaneda, *The Eagle's Gift*, Penguin Arkana (1992), p 8, 40.
— The new seers call the emphasised emanations
Carlos Castaneda, *The Fire From Within*, GB: Black Swan (1984), p 159.

CHAPTER ELEVEN: TALKING TO GHOSTS
— I was shocked awake by a feathered wing
Michael Harner, *Cave and Cosmos: Shamanic Encounters with Another Reality*, Berkeley: North Atlantic Books, 2013, p 18.
— They described sightings of ghostly strangers
— Rumiko was slumped
Richard Lloyd Parry, *Ghosts of the Tsunami*, London Review of Books, Vol. 36 No. 3, 6 February 2014.

— Ok, now what do I do?
Transcription, AgapeSchoolinz meditation group meeting, 10 April 2014.
— What are all you people doing here?
Ibid, 30 January, 2014.

CHAPTER TWELVE: SPOOKY STUFF AT A DISTANCE

— We grant there are possible spooky worlds
David Lewis, 'What Experience Teaches' in *The Nature of Consciousness: Philosophical Debates*, The MIT Press (1997), p 585.
— The mind is a self-organising republic
Edward O. Wilson, *Consilience*, London: Abacus (1998), p 120.

Recommended Reading

HISTORICAL ESOTERICISM, MYSTICISM, OCCULTISM, MAGIC

Geoffrey Ashe
The Ancient Wisdom, London: MacMillan (1971)
Anne Bancroft
Origins of the Sacred: The Spiritual Journey in Western Tradition, Arkana (1987)
Paul Brunton
A Search in Sacred India, London: Rider (1934)
Timothy Freke & Peter Gandy
The Hermetica: The Lost Wisdom of the Pharaohs, Tarcher (2008)
E.J. Holmyard
Alchemy, NY: Dover (1957)
Idries Shah
Oriental Magic, London: Octagon Press (1956)
Evelyn Underhill
Mysticism: A Study of the Nature and Development of Man's Spiritual Consciousness, NY: E.P. Dutton (1961, originally published 1913)
Frances Yates
Giordano Bruno and the Hermetic Tradition, London: Routledge and Kegan Paul (1964)
The Occult Philosophy in the Elizabethan Age, London: Routledge and Kegan Paul (1979)

CONTEMPORARY MYSTICISM AND ANOMALOUS PERCEPTIONS

Eben Alexander, M.D.
Proof of Heaven: A Neurosurgeon's Journey into the Afterlife, NY: Simon and Schuster (2012)
William Buhlman
Adventures Beyond the Body, San Fransisco: HarperOne (1996)
The Secret of the Soul, Harper-San Fransisco (2001)

Chris Carter
Science and the Near-Death Experience: How Consciousness Survives Death, Inner Traditions (2010)
Science and Psychic Phenomena: The Fall of the House of Sceptics, Inner Traditions (2nd ed., 2012)
Larry Dossey M.D.
Reinventing Medicine: Beyond Body-Mind to a New Era of Healing, Harper-SanFransisco (2000)
Robert K.C. Foreman
Grassroots Spirituality: What It Is, Why It Is Here, Where It Is Going, Imprint Academic (2004)
Joseph McMoneagle
Remote Viewing Secrets, Hampton Roads Publishing Co., (2000)
The Stargate Chronicles: Memoirs of a Psychic Spy, Crossroad Press (E-book edition, 2014)
Charles Tart
The End of Materialism, New Harbinger Publications, (2009)
Ken Wilber
A Brief History of Everything, Boston: Shambhala (2000)
The Marriage of Sense and Soul: Integrating Science and Religion, NY: Broadway Books (1998)

SHAMANISM: ANCIENT AND CONTEMPORARY

Carlos Castaneda
The Teachings of Don Juan: A Yaqui Way of Knowledge, University of California Press (1968)
A Separate Reality, NY: Simon and Schuster (1971)
Journey to Ixtlan, NY: Simon and Schuster (1972)
Mircea Eliade
Shamanism: Archaic Techniques of Ecstasy, Princeton University Press (1964)
Michael Harner
Cave and Cosmos: Shamanic Encounters with Another Reality, North Atlantic Books (2013)

Index